D0093561

As you walk through the valley of the unknown, you will find footprints of Jesus both in front of you and beside you.

Charles Stanley

Wisdom for the Road Ahead
Walking with God While Walking on Campus

By Adam Erwin

Ace Publishing, Inc.

ACE Publishing, Inc.

Published in Minneapolis, Minnesota, by Ace Publishing, Inc.

Book Design by Andrea Gillette

Printed in the United States of America
ISBN 0-9721774-1-8

TABLE OF CONTENTS

Chapter 4
What to Expect in the Classroom

Chapter 5
Will You Pass the Dating Test?

Chapter 6
Family and Friends: How to Keep Up with Those You've Left Behind

Chapter 7
Living Arrangements: Where to Live Out Your Faith

Acknowledgements

It seems that only at the end of a long journey does one have the perspective from which to best appreciate the splendor of their travels. As this book goes to print, I can now understand and perhaps smile at the great pains and frustrations God had in store for me while working on this project. To quote a phrase from the Caedmon's Call tune "Lead of Love": "I had to walk the rocks to see the mountain view, looking back I see the lead of love." Praise God for what He had to do in me to get these words through me. He has proven time and again to be my Rock, my Provider, and my Strength. Although I am hopeful that many will learn from this book, I confess that I may have been taught the most. May God be praised and may others be blessed by the work of worship in the pages ahead.

Annie Gillette, you are a special talent. In addition to putting up with my horrible combination of perfectionist and procrastinator, you calmly deliver under pressure. Thanks for your cover work and layout. And thanks for doing this for free! Just kidding, check's in the mail.

The names of the hundreds of high school seniors, college students, youth pastors, and college ministry workers who have shared their stories, advice, fears, and prayers for this book are too numerous to mention. You know who you are. Second to God's word, your contributions are the highlight of this book. Thank you!

I have been sent many great helpers to work closely on this project. Without the help of these editors/encouragers, this book would remain on the list of "things I should have done for the Lord." Many thanks to the following folks: David

Sanford, Bethany Goodrow, Jenni Marken, Elizabeth Ries, Joe Summers, Gabriel Zeigler, Tim Sawyer, Dharma Amundsen, Abby Ludvigson, Beth Eppinger, Meaghan Phelan, Brian Schulenberg, Nicole Nelson, Ann McNiece, and Carole and Steve Treichler.

Charlie Schaller, thanks so much for your kind foreword. You graciously put the demands of this project ahead of your own commitments. Thanks for your great heart and attitude of servanthood. You are a great example and student of the Faith. Bless you!

To my roommates Chris, Jeff, and Gabe: Thanks for allowing God to use you to teach and grow me through our interactions. Without your accountability, availability, and encouragement, I would be a much lesser person.

To Karen, Ben, and baby Christian: Although I am blessed by watching your marriage and family grow, I am more blessed by your encouragement. I cannot properly fashion the words to express my appreciation for your uplifting presence in my life. I thank God for sending me a great sister, a new brother, and a joy of a nephew.

To Mom: I can only imagine how many hours you have prayed for me over these past twelve months. Even though it'd be nice to be home, I can easily feel your love from ten hours away. You are a gift to me from God.

To Mr. Rue: You are so good to me. Whether we laugh or weep together, I am continually blessed by my time with you. It seems like all you do is serve others. I could call you Tony, step-dad, mentor, friend, or my great cheerleader. But to me, "Buddy" encapsulates all of those just fine.

To Fran: I've learned much about your character these past few years. In the midst of recent trials, you have risen with grace and strength to meet the situation as it has called for.

Thanks for loving me, my sister, and my dad so much. I love you!

To Dad: As I sat in the waiting room during your heart surgery, these words from Dan Folgerberg's song "Leader of the Band" came to mind: "I thank you for the music and your stories of the road. I thank you for the freedom when it came my time to go. I thank you for the kindness and the times when you've gone tough. And papa I don't think I've said I love you near enough." Between a quintuple bypass and colon cancer, I cannot remember the last time I so passionately cried over you, prayed for you, or fainted before you (literally!). I'm grateful God decided to keep you around. I love you, Daddy! Thanks for your generous provision for this book.

Foreword

As you crack open this book for the first time and flip through its pages, I can't help but feel a sense of excitement for you. You may be sitting at your kitchen table next to a large stack of blank "Thank You" notes owed to the guests of your graduation open house. It may be the first night of college. You sit awake in your new bed while, across the dark room a complete stranger whom you will spend the next nine months living with, sleeps soundly. Regardless of where you are right now, one fact remains: You have absolutely no idea what you are in for…

While I don't doubt that many of you about to read this book are, like me, already in college, a far greater number of you are poised on the edge of the great precipice that is high school graduation. If I may offer one piece of consolation to those ready for life to end come September, it is that yes, the world does continue past your 18th year. Despite what the sappy songs and tearful goodbyes suggest, this is not the end of love, laughter and friendship.

College is not simply the end of high school. It is an amazing place, filled with new experiences, emotions, and relationships. During your time at college you will obtain a wealth of knowledge. I estimate that no more than 20 percent of it will be achieved in the classroom. While this is indeed a time to learn about calculus, organic chemistry, or Shakespeare, it is equally a time to learn about confronting your fears, finding your passions, and growing in your relationship with God.

One of the greatest fallacies that I've encountered on the college campus is this: to learn more about the world or yourself you must leave God behind. This logic is flawed. If indeed God is the creator of all things good and beautiful, then I can suggest no better guide to this new world of your adult life than the Lord.

And that is why this book has been written: to inform and prepare you for the challenges of college, both minor and significant, while keeping your eyes on Jesus, the great Professor. As this book heads to press, over two hundred and fifty college students have had a hand in its creation. This book is intended as a ministry. It is a compilation of experiences, victories, and defeats intended to make your own college walk a bit more illuminated, if not easier.

During my years at the University of Minnesota, one of the largest secular campuses in the world, I have seen spiritual giants crumble and spiritual weaklings rise to demonstrate great strength. And as you are preparing to leave college in four years (or five or six...), you will look back on your undergraduate years and fall into one of two groups. You will see your college years as either a time where you: 1) became closer and stronger in your relationship with God or 2) grew distanced and weaker. I have not yet seen one exception to this rule. Decide earnestly and quickly with which group you wish to belong, because each is reached through conscious and deliberate decisions.

I am certain that you have had your fill of cliché analogies, so I won't tell you that there comes a time when each little bird must leave the nest, or each tugboat must to go to sea. I will tell you, though, that each little bird is going into a strange, hostile new world full of bigger birds and each tugboat is going to have to weather its share of storms before it finds safe harbors. It is my prayer that this book will be a blessing to you as you encounter the inevitable challenges ahead. Be nervous, be scared, be prayerful, but be excited! You are about to enter a new world. Do so with a hopeful and expectant heart.

And never put a wool sweater in the dryer.

-Charlie Schaller

A knowledge of the Bible without a college course is more valuable than a college course without the Bible.

Unknown

Introduction

The longest drive of my life took place a few years ago in August. I was on the way from my home in St. Louis, Missouri to the University of Minnesota, located in Minneapolis, MN. I was excited, fearful, nervous, apprehensive, and ambitious all at once. Although I had visited the campus that April, I had no idea what the residence halls would be like, how the food would taste, what the classes would be like, and who my friends would be. It was a school of approximately 40,000 students. I knew no one and no one knew me.

What about my roommate? Would we get along? Would my relationship with my girlfriend from home really last? What about my faith in God? Would I live it out or choose, like some Christians, to put it aside during college? Was I going to procrastinate the way I did in high school and just try to "get by" with projects and tests? Would I feel alone?

My brain was flooded with questions as I made it to campus that first day. A little more than four years later, I've got more answers and more stories than I have time to share them. I have answers now to questions I didn't know to ask as a freshman. Having pulled more than a few all-nighters and having mastered the caffeine high, I leave college with a degree and the most priceless of all educations: life experience.

If there is one thing experience teaches us, it's this: We learn in the end what we wanted to know in the beginning. I have the insight as a college graduate that I wish I would've had as a freshman. I now know how important it is to surround yourself right away with people who make you better instead of choosing those who pressure you to become lesser. I understand how right C.S. Lewis was when he said, "Either the Bible will keep you away from sin, or sin will keep you away from the Bible." And it has finally clicked in my head that doing homework is not punishment but actually an act of worship. At one time college seemed so complicated and now it seems much simpler. After four and a half years of college and two degrees, I'm finally ready for my freshman year!

However, freshman year is a once-in-a-lifetime experience, and I've already had my one shot. It was a wonderful and crazy experience. And now it's your turn. But before you take your first strides down the road of college, I'd like to spend some time with you and equip you with the answers to your most burning questions. Perhaps you have questions about what to expect in the residence halls, how to avoid temptations, what not to fear, what to be aware of, what to do, and what not to do. You may even be feeling as if you don't know what questions to ask. The number of questions you have is not as important as your willingness to listen to tested and God-centered wisdom for the road ahead.

What This Book Offers: Advice from This Generation

"Don't drink anything out of the punch bowl at the fraternity parties!" my mother warned me one summer day before my freshman year of college. "You never know if it's spiked," she added.

I didn't know much about college at that time, but I did

know that there wouldn't be punch bowls at any parties. I knew my mom was full of advice about college, but she had attended more than twenty years before me. By her even mentioning the punch bowl, I knew I wouldn't be able to get much relevant advice from her. For that matter, none of the aunts, uncles, and other educated adults I knew could offer advice I was willing to listen to. Even my youth pastor's college experience was, well…dated.

There had to be someone close to my age that had sound college advice for me, right? My sister was in the middle of her college experience, living in our hometown and attending Saint Louis University, a private school of 12,000 students. I was moving ten hours away and attending a public school of 40,000 students. I was sure her circumstances were much different from the ones I would face. Therefore, I didn't think I could count on her for accurate advice.

In addition, most of the advice I was getting was coming from people who went to colleges that were a different size, in a different state, or that had a different focus or atmosphere compared with my school. Most of the advice came from people who could not remotely relate to what I would soon be experiencing.

If you are entering college soon, you may be having a tough time gathering wisdom about the road ahead. A little advice about what to do and what not to do would be helpful, but it's hard to find someone who really knows what you'll be experiencing.

This book is a compilation of advice from over two hundred Christian students who are either in school or graduating as this goes to print. These students hail from all over the nation, from Maine to Malibu. They attend Ivy League institutions, Big Ten universities, Christian colleges, and technical schools. I have interviewed everyone from athletes to law students to finance majors to pharmaceutical students.

Wisdom for the Road Ahead is full of God-centered ideas and suggestions about what to do from day one of college so that you can get the most out of your experience. When interviewing college students for this book, I asked each person this question: "If you had 30 minutes to spend with high school seniors, what would you tell them about college?" Some people launched into hour-long conversations about the best and worst of their experiences. There were things they would change, things they would keep, and things they would add to their college experiences. In the pages ahead I provide many of their true stories about experiences that shaped them.

This guide will provide some shortcuts and also hard lessons learned by all kinds of students. If you keep the ideas of this book in mind while you are at school, you can have an easier time in the classroom, a more exciting time outside the classroom, and avoid all the wrong steps that can derail one's faith and even damage lives.

The result of this research is a Christian guide to success in ten different areas of college living. This is not a "catchall" for what is to be or should be experienced in college. It is, however, a set of Biblically-based principles that will fit almost anyone headed to college. My intention is to help future college students, as well as the parents and loved ones of future college students, get a fresh perspective on the road ahead.

Perhaps the most valuable aspect of this book is timing.

As I reflect on my life's journey thus far, college has not even registered in my rearview mirror yet. I chose to write this book now because the insight provided here comes from people who are still experiencing college and have a clear idea of which strategies in college living work effectively and which ones do not. Memories are fresh, ideas are concrete, and examples have not been exaggerated by the passing of time. I pray that this book will provide useful wisdom to help any college student along their faith and education journey, regardless of their destination.

The winds of God are always blowing, but you must set the sails.

Unknown

Chapter 7

Independence: How to Experience Freedom Without Falling Victim to It

Heading to college is like traveling a new road. One may not know exactly where to go or what to expect, but there are bound to be once-in-a-lifetime opportunities, chances to meet new friends, and additional responsibilities. It's not just the start of another semester or a new school year, it is quite possibly the first time in your life when you get to call the shots. A new-found load of independence weighs squarely on your shoulders. How will you handle this new-found freedom? More importantly, how will it affect your walk with Christ?

Some Christians thrive when delivered into independence, others falter in their faith. Many Christians choose to turn away from their faith during college, in a sense trading their walk with God for their life on campus. Clearly, freedom is a dangerous thing. Either you will be dangerous for the Lord or dangerous to yourself. This chapter provides helpful travel tips for the road of college and sheds light on the tricky parts of the path of independence where many students take a wrong turn.

Know Who You Are... And Who You're Not

In college, independence is the starting point of the complex process of finding one's identity. Most students are in the process of trying to figure out who they are, and the temptation is to try any and every experience to see if it fits them. Even some of the most seemingly solid Christian students will "try on" alcohol or "try on" sex as if they were trying on different costumes. One of the great challenges of college for many students is putting the Christian life into practice. It is not something you put on, it is worn from the inside. It's the difference between playing a role and living out an identity. By that, I mean that who you are and the things you do should not be left to chance. A solid identity in Christ means that in any given circumstance your decisions are pre-set so that they do not waiver. Let me share a couple of stories about people who learned first-hand the importance of setting pre-determined standards.

As a freshman at the University of Minnesota, I was curious about the party scene. I wanted to experience a fraternity party or two, go to a house party perhaps, and see why everyone hyped up the weekend life on campus. Although I wasn't pursuing God passionately at the time, I was fortunate that He had instilled some immovable concrete barriers in my lifestyle: No alcohol, no sex, and no drugs. Those three were never an option.

One Friday night a few weeks into my first semester, about ten guys from my residence hall decided to go hit up the biggest frat party on campus. When we arrived it was packed and everyone was either playing a drinking game or dancing. It felt like fourteen MTV videos rolled into one party!

After embarrassing myself on the dance floor, I left my friends and drifted over to check out a particular drinking game. Within minutes I was asked to join. I quickly declined the invitation. Five minutes later, I was asked again to join. I refused and told everyone that I really didn't drink. Finally, the group pooled together $100 to have me taste some alcohol. I stood my ground, said no, and left frat house. To this day, "no alcohol" is still an immovable barrier in my life.

"So this is the big party scene?" I asked myself as I walked back to the residence halls. I failed to see what all the hype was about. It was as if I had journeyed to Oz, pulled back the curtain to get a glimpse of the wizard, and was very unimpressed by what I saw.

Kyle, who attends the University of Missouri, made different decisions at frat parties. At his first party, he had a couple of drinks. The very next night he got drunk. In fact, he drank heavily three nights a week for his entire freshman year. As a result, his grades suffered horribly and he began to have serious liver problems (probably more genetically-related than alcohol-related, but still!). The worst and most blatant outcome of his bout with alcohol was that he compromised his identity. His friends knew him to be a heavy drinker and had no idea that he was a believer. Kyle didn't feel like a believer, either. He felt so distanced from God that it took him more than a year without alcohol to feel truly alive as a Christian again.

Kyle and I faced the same identity test with very different results. It is solely by the grace of God that I did not compromise my identity as a Christian to try on the costume of heavy drinking. Even in my apparent "triumph", I did some dumb things that I would like to steer you away from. Here are a few ideas to take to heart when faced with tests of your identity during college.

Set immovable barriers in your lifestyle! In college, your actions are the best indicator of who you are trying to be. Therefore, set immovable concrete barriers in your lifestyle that will clearly establish your Christian beliefs. Write down and share with some friends the things you will make an effort to do daily (read the Bible, spend time in prayer, serve others) to show who you are. Likewise, make a list of things that you are sincerely committed to avoid in order to reveal who you're not. And lastly, don't forget that you are an imperfect human. If you reach a moment when you compromise one of your barriers, ask for forgiveness, turn away from your sin, and move on. You won't ever be perfect, that is God's job. Your immovable barriers are just a way to help you do your best in living out an identity consistent with your beliefs.

Always stay with the pack! I did one of the stupidest things possible that night at the frat party...I isolated myself from my friends. And to top it off, the friends I chose to party with were not Christians! Instead of adhering to the advice of 1 Corinthians 15:33 which warns, "Bad company corrupts good character," I went into an environment where I was surrounded by sin. And I had no one there to hold me accountable. Not very smart on my part!

We are most susceptible when we are by ourselves and Satan knows this. If you are entering into testy waters (and I pray that you will seek God's wisdom to avoid such circumstances), know that isolating yourself will produce the greatest opportunity for temptation. If Satan tempted the Son of Man when Jesus was alone in Matthew chapter 4, he won't hesitate to go after you too. The bottom line is this: when we know temptation is coming, it is important to surround ourselves with friends who can help us hold fast to our identity in Christ.

Learn to flee! According to Merriam-Webster's dictionary, flee means to "escape danger or evil." It is not a matter of being a coward and choosing not to rise up to a challenge. Rather, fleeing is directly linked to temptation. In times when you know your identity is being tested, be quick to flee. When I was being invited to drink at the party, I was very slow to flee. I admit that my curiosity peaked a little more each time I was asked to partake. When temptation runs toward you, run away from it. Paul gives the following instructions in 2 Timothy 2:22, "Flee the evil desires of youth, and pursue righteousness, faith, love, and peace, along with those who call on the Lord out of a pure heart." The Bible also says in James 4:7, "Submit yourselves, then, to God. Resist the devil, and he will flee from you." Immediately flee whenever temptation is mounting an attack on your identity.

As we wrap up this section it is important to clarify that this discussion is about challenging scenarios, not just about alcohol. Granted, the Bible warns us in Proverbs 20:1, "Wine is a mocker and beer a brawler; whoever is led astray by them is not wise." And although I do not choose to drink, the Bible doesn't condemn it in moderation when one is lawfully of age to do so. Heck, Jesus drank wine from time to time.

Battles for your identity and integrity can come from most anywhere: in the classroom, at a party, on the internet, at your part-time job. Setting immovable lifestyle barriers, staying with the pack, and learning to flee will help you live out your identity in Christ.

Be Smart with Your Schedule

College provides the opportunity you've been waiting for your entire life: the chance to sleep until 3p.m. everyday! Contrast that to what Ben Franklin said in *Poor Richards Almanac*, "Early to bed, and early to rise, makes a man healthy, wealthy, and wise." Given the extreme hours that characterize much of today's college life, I don't think Mr. Franklin ever lived in a residence hall. The idea behind the quote is important, though. There are many benefits to being smart with your schedule.

My friend Mike was not an adept scheduler his freshman year. Going to school at the University of Michigan, he scheduled an 8 a.m. class that met on the opposite side of campus. "God did not create me to be a morning person," he said. "I was not into getting up at 7:30 five days a week. It was so stinking cold at 8 a.m. that it wasn't worth the long walk. And I'm a night owl too. Since there was never enough coffee on the planet to keep me up early in the mornings I always fell asleep. For me, the question became: Do I stay in bed and sleep here or get dressed and sleep in class?"

Mike certainly learned a lesson about how not to schedule classes. Being a guy who thinks better at night, it wasn't a great idea to schedule a class early in the morning. He's not alone in being a casualty of the clock. Most students will not only struggle with planning out classes, but also wrestle with how to best fill the rest of their day.

Have you ever reached the end of a lazy day only to feel as if you totally wasted it? Of course you have! That's because God created in us a need to be good stewards of the time He gives us. Here are some ways to make sure you are working with time and not against it.

Get up at a reasonable hour everyday. If you don't want to waste your day, don't sleep it away. Scripture tabs Jesus as an early riser in Mark 1:35. Getting up at a consistent time everyday provides your body with the structure it needs to function properly.

Commit your day to a schedule. Have you ever seen someone receive a gift that he or she had no intention of using? God gives us the gift of time everyday. I can only imagine how frustrating it would be to consistently award twenty-four hours to a person who wastes the majority of it. Before you go to bed at night, I challenge you to create a schedule for the following day. Try it for a week and see how much you accomplish. You'll be amazed at how complete your days can be when you honor the time God provides you.

Go for the "Less is More" approach. Freshman year is like having training wheels on your bike. You will get around alright, but you won't be able to go as fast as you'd like and it can be awkward when making turns. While you get adjusted to college life, schedule less activities with more time to get each one done.

Most students struggle with time management during college and beyond. You will be amazed how often the excuse "I don't have time" surfaces on a college campus. Ironically enough, God gave each one of us the same amount of time in each day. And being one of the many resources He has given us, God calls us to be good stewards of our time. The only way to truly appreciate this gift is to maximize it. Be smart with your schedule!

The Battle of Loneliness on Campus

I have talked with hundreds of college freshmen, and one of their greatest fears is that of being lonely. What if you don't make any friends? What good is it to have freedom if you don't have anyone to spend your time with? You might be surprised how at many incoming freshman worry about meeting people and making friends.

Kari, who attends Iowa State University, was afraid she would never find friends like the ones back home. "I was scared because, starting out, I didn't know too many people on my campus," she said. "All of the friends I had from high school were either living at home or were living in a dorm all the way across campus. I just left my door open every day and hoped for the best. Things couldn't have turned out better."

Here's the thing about being a freshman: Everyone is in it together. The residence halls are a great place to be because most freshman are experiencing similar things, and everyone seems to struggle with the same types of worries. Meeting people is a lot easier in college (especially freshman year) because everyone can connect with your daily triumphs and trials.

God created us with a need for fellowship and community. He would not have created us this way if He had no plans to fulfill it. If you are concerned about meeting people, I encourage you to do three things: 1) pray everyday for God to bring good people into your life, 2) invite people to eat meals with you, and 3) don't isolate yourself in your room. Seek out a Christian organization on campus, go to play sports at the rec center, or even venture out to a local coffee shop. Meeting people, especially freshman year, is easier than you may believe. When you really think about it, loneliness is a choice. Keep an open door and an open mind. Just remember that you are not alone.

Never Put a Wool Sweater in the Dryer!

A month into my freshman year I bought this expensive wool sweater from J. Crew. I loved this sweater like no other. It was my favorite piece of my wardrobe. Who am I kidding, *it was my wardrobe.* Anyway, I went out one night, and some guy ran into me and dumped his triple heartburn nachos and overflowing cup of cheap brew right onto my new sweater. Perhaps it was his way of sharing. Seeing this as an opportunity to put my patience and resourcefulness to task, I decided to wash my sweater the very next day.

I ran it through the washer with no problem. Even though I had many questions about fabrics at the time, I decided a dry sweater was better than a wet one, so I put the sweater in the dryer. I came back fifty minutes later to find myself holding up a wool tank top. I spent the whole day trying to stretch that baby back to size. I'm thinking of giving the sweater to my cousin sometime soon. He's six.

I learned a very expensive lesson thanks to my sweater: always ask when you have a question. Like many students, I got in a jam and was too proud and too cowardly to ask for help. Part of being independent is realizing that we're always in some way dependent. When in a tough spot, take courage, put on humility, and ask for help.

You may be wondering, "Who should I go to when I have a question or am in a predicament?" If your parents aren't available or most suitable, there are Community Advisors/Residential Assistants in every residence hall to answer questions about campus living, the bus system, laundry, and almost anything else. There are also academic advisors, mental health counselors, and various other people on campus. They are there to help you. Ask them for it! There are tons of resources for any question you may have. The trick is to ask.

Making the Most of Your Independence

Independence is a double-edged sword: you can use it to better yourself or you can choose to have it be a powerful tool used towards your detriment. Using your independence wisely involves knowing who you are, being smart with your schedule, opening yourself up to the opportunity of meeting new people, and being brave enough to ask questions. Use your independence wisely. It's worth the effort.

Freedom is first of all a responsibility before the God from whom we come.

Alan Keyes

Anything that dims my vision for Christ, or takes away my taste for Bible study, or cramps me in my prayer life, or makes Christian work difficult, is wrong for me; and I must, as a Christian turn away from it.

J. Wilbur Chapman

Chapter 2

Making Faith a Priority: Essentials for Building a Strong Foundation

Have you ever driven through the southeast portion of Colorado? If you have, you may recall two very contrasting images as you travel: 1) tumbleweeds roaming about aimlessly, and 2) an occasional stream with bountiful vegetation on its banks.

You will see this very scene on your college campus. Some students will wander aimlessly like the tumbleweed, with a withered and dried out faith (if they have any faith at all), seemingly blown by the wind in any direction. Yet, students who have a faith rooted deeply in the Lord can be seen right on the banks of His waters, growing stronger and living with joy amidst the beauty of a needed stream. Psalms 1: 3 says this of the man who takes delight in the law of the LORD, "He is like a tree planted by streams of water, which yields its fruits in season and whose leaf does not wither. Whatever he does prospers." Each campus will have the water of Life running through it. How does a student get rooted in God's presence on campus and find their way to the stream that brings lasting life?

The Most Important Search: Finding a Good Church

Did you grow up going to the same church for many years? Is there a particular youth group or youth pastor that helped you grow and encouraged you during your high school years? When I left for college as a freshman, I wanted to take my Evangelical Free Church, youth group, and youth pastor with me. I couldn't imagine things being the same at a new church. How was I supposed to find a group as cool as the one I had at my home church?

When I arrived on campus at the University of Minnesota for the first time, I was so surprised and blessed to meet some friends who were eager to look for a church to attend. When Sunday rolled around, we met in the middle of campus and proceeded like a small herd of lost sheep, wandering about in search of a suitable looking church. We walked around for an hour (baaahh!) before we found what seemed to be a good fit. We clumsily found the way to our seats just as service was beginning.

The service was awful! The hymns were sung out of tune, the sermon was hard to follow, not to mention incredibly boring. Various prayers and ceremonies were carried out without any passion whatsoever. There was, however, one saving grace....excellent pastries afterward! What that church was missing during the service was made up for with some of the best baked goods that I've ever enjoyed. These pastries were like a combination of the best breads from around the world. We're talking Krispy Kreme doughnuts meets Olive Garden breadsticks!

As I was working on my fourth pastry (nothing like chowing down on free food!), I wandered over to a massive bulletin board that had caught my eye. An article was posted front and center of it and I began to read. I can't recall the exact words of the article, but the main idea went something like this: The Bible is such a big book and it's impossible to apply everything in it, so just pay attention to the parts that make sense to you. I was shocked! What type of church is this, I wondered? Absolutely nothing about this church ministered to me. I knew at that moment that I would not ever be able to worship there again. Frustrated and confused, I joined my fellow lost sheep and we ventured back toward campus (baahhhh!).

It took me months to find a good church. In fact, I spent many Sunday mornings sleeping in, too frustrated to search for a place to worship. Once I found a solid church (which happened to be all of 200 feet from my residence hall), I couldn't get enough of it. The services of Hope Community Church were held late in the morning (sleep is good), the music rocked, the teachings were very Biblical, and it was full of college students. I've been attending Hope for six years now! Praise the Lord for providing me with such a fitting house of praise.

So, what's the best way to find a new church home in college? I spoke with a very popular youth pastor in Atlanta about how to find a good church on campus. Here's what Mike recommended:

1) **Find out where other students attend**-"I encourage the students who are headed toward college to go online and find out which Christian groups are on campus," explained Mike. "From there, email one of the staff members in each campus group and ask where most of the students in that group attend church. This way, freshmen will have a nice list of churches to try out that other students like. It's always nice to have options right off the bat."

2) **Be open to a new worship experience**-"Most students are looking for a church that is exactly like theirs at home, but no two churches are the same," advises Mike. "It's important to be open to a new kind of worship experience because God might want to reach you in a new way." There are many ways to learn about and worship the Lord. Some students make the mistake of looking for a church with a certain worship style instead of focusing on finding a church that has strong Biblically based teaching. Be open to a new worship experience, but don't compromise the importance of Biblical teaching in the process.

3) **Be persistent in the search for your new church**-Sad but true, many students will just stop searching for a church after awhile. According to Mike, students must stay the course and search hard for a place of worship. "I encourage students to go every Sunday to a new church until they find one they like. A community of fellowship is incredibly important during college. God will honor full-hearted diligence in search of a place to worship Him."

Jenni, one of my extraordinary student editors, offered this piece of insight: "It's important to understand the difference between attending a church and getting involved in a church."

That's right on target! You see, those who attend a church are usually getting poured into, but those who are involved are also being poured out through. It is important to offer your gifts, talents, and time in order to be an active member of the body of Christ. "If you like kids," Jenni continued, "help in the nursery or teach Sunday school. Musically talented? Sing in the choir or play with the worship team. Either way, offer your services."

It is incredibly important to find a place to call your church home. If you can learn where other Christian students attend, are open to a new worship experience, and are persistent in your pursuit of a place of worship, God will bless your search. God desires your worship, praise, and fellowship. I pray that you will search diligently for a place to meet with Him.

Big and Small: The Need for Christian Fellowship in Many Sizes

Sarah studies psychology at Miami University in Oxford, Ohio. One of her major faith goals the first week of her freshman year was to find a Christian group on campus. Fliers had been posted all over campus by several Christian groups and Sarah soon realized she had many options to choose from. From the minute she walked into Bachelor Hall to attend her first InterVarsity Bustaway weekly meeting (large group meeting, that is), Sarah felt at home.

"It just kinda clicked right away," she said. "They had everything I was looking for: we met as a big group, had small group bible studies, and went off on retreats and stuff. I couldn't have asked for more.

"God blessed me so much with such a great group of friends, and my relationship with Him grew so much. Big group (Bustaway meeting) was good because I could get lost in worship and also hear a cool message about Jesus. I liked small group Bible studies because I was able to really learn about how to live like Jesus in my daily life. And the retreats rocked because I could get away and really connect with God, not to mention having the chance to deepen some awesome friendships.

"If I could sit down with an incoming freshman who wants to grow their faith," Sarah continued, "I'd tell them to keep their eyes peeled for a Christian group on their campus that offers a big group meeting, a small group meeting, and a chance to go on retreats. It is a great challenge to live out the Christian faith on a college campus. Incoming freshmen will want to have many opportunities, big and small, to worship and fellowship."

Sarah is on target with her recommendations. I strongly encourage you to pursue a group that can help feed you spiritually in a big and small group setting.

Quiet Times: Refreshment in your Day

Do you eat everyday? I do! Our bodies have a need to be nourished each day in order for us to function properly. God has created in us a similar need for daily spiritual nourishment, yet many Christians don't seem to consistently tend to this hunger. On every college campus there are countless challenges and spiritual battles. Without proper food for the soul, we are too weak for life on the Christian path. For this reason, daily time in God's word is a must in college.

To be open with you, I didn't know about the importance of spending daily time with God until my sophomore year in college. One day during my second year at Minnesota I was fumbling around in the Bible. I came across Luke 6:12, which talks about Jesus praying all night to God. It hit me at that moment that if Jesus, the Son of Man, decided to spend daily quiet time with God, then I should also make an effort to spend time with God everyday (Mark 1:35, John 8:1-2, Matt. 11:28-29, and Matt. 14: 23 are also examples of Jesus spending one-on-one time with God).

Mark, a youth pastor in Denver, says that the best thing any student can do is get in the habit of reading their Bible everyday. "The jump from youth group to college is so huge that it's essential to spend time with God day in and day out. In college you have to learn how to live your faith....not just learning about what Jesus did, but learning to live like Jesus. Jesus spent time with God daily, and students need to do the same."

Daily time with God is not an exact science. There is no specific formula for what works best. Many of the students I interviewed recommend trying to put together some combination of the following ideas to find a rhythm in your time with God.

1) **Find a quiet place**-Since God is the most important thing in the universe, why not treat Him like it? It is essential to find a place where you can turn off the cell phone, step away from instant messaging, and free yourself from the distractions of the world.

2) **Invite God to join you**-Ever felt lost when starting a prayer or when reading the Bible? Maybe you don't know how or where to start, or finish. By inviting God to be with you, you open up your senses to Him. Ask Him to speak to your

ears, to guide your eyes, and tug at your heart. He desires to enter into a time of close fellowship with you, why not invite Him daily?

3) **Get into God's word**-The Bible is full of God's wisdom, greatness, and promises. The everyday trials of life require us to study God's word and take root in it. Whether it is a program where you read the Bible in a year or have an assignment from you small group Bible study, get into the Word. Even if you start off by spending just a few minutes with God, that's a great first step.

"A quiet time with God does for my spirit what sleep does for my body," says Marquis, a junior at Virginia Tech. "When I don't spend time with the Lord, it's like I've gone without sleep. I'm not as sharp, not as kind, and not as connected with what God is trying to do around me and in me. If you want to feel close to God, spend time with Him."

Nothing has been more important to building my faith as daily time spent with God. It is not always an easy thing to do, but it is certainly worth your effort. If you are looking for a way to feel refreshed, centered, and ready for what the world throws at you, start by spending time with God on a daily basis.

Accountability: How to Get Away with Nothing

I remember it like it was yesterday. It was a perfect fall evening during my sophomore year. Matt and I were walking back to the residence halls after Realife, the weekly meeting at the University of Minnesota for Campus Crusade for Christ. I remember our conversation that night was a long one: sports, relationships, cars, class, God…it was a deep and steady exchange for at least fifteen minutes, which can be a long time for guys. When we reached the commons right outside my room, Matt looked me square in the eye and asked, "Adam, would you be my accountability partner?"

"Dude, what do you need that for? You aren't taking any accounting classes," I replied, totally clueless as to what he was asking.

"No, dude. It's not for class. An accountability partner is someone you get together with every week," Matt explained. "It's someone you pray with and pray for, a person you share your sins and struggles with, someone you can trust and be totally open with. I want us to help each other grow in faith. One of the Campus Crusade staff leaders encouraged me to get an accountability partner, and I'd like it to be you."

I was kind of surprised by the request, but was impressed with the courage it took to ask for that type of honesty and trust out of one another. "I'm in, for sure," I said. "Let's start tomorrow. We'll meet for lunch at noon."

The very next day we began what would be one of the most difficult and rewarding processes of faith growth during college. Once a week, Matt and I would find a quiet place to share our bouts with everything from purity to procrastination. We would pray together during that time (and for each other everyday in between), we'd ask tough questions, and share answers openly and honestly. Each time I'd walk away from my meeting with Matt feeling encouraged, relieved, and focused on God.

It is a really, really good idea to consider getting an accountability partner during your first year of college. "I don't

43

know what I would've done without having Nicole in my life," Carrie said. "It was hard enough being a first-year student at Northwestern University. There was so much on my mind, and I was having trouble letting go of some of the things in my life that were bringing me down. If it wasn't for accountability with Nicole, I'm not sure I would've grown in my faith the way I did."

You might be thinking, "How do I go about getting an accountability partner?" Here are ideas the experts suggested as a possible route to finding someone who can help you grow in your faith.

1) **Pray**-Pray daily for God to bring someone into your life that you can relate to and with whom you feel comfortable.

2) **Be on the look out**-Whether it is at church or with a Christian group on campus, keep your eyes peeled for a student who has a strong faith. You will want to be paired up with someone who will encourage you in your walk with God. Be wary of someone who seems to be deeply struggling in their relationship with Jesus.

3) **Avoid cross-gender accountability**-This one is crucial: don't pursue accountability with someone of the opposite sex. Men and women are wired differently and can have vastly different areas of struggle. Therefore, it can be difficult to truly relate and understand exactly what a person of the opposite sex is going through. In addition, sometimes attraction between the man and woman can get in the way of talking effectively and openly about sins and struggles. Make sure to stay away from members of the opposite sex when it comes to accountability.

4) **Ask for help in the hunt**-Whether it is a staff member of

a Christian group on campus or a pastor at your church, it's okay to ask for help in finding an accountability partner. These people may be able to recommend activities where you can get to know other students a little better, or perhaps they will have someone in mind that might be a good fit for you.

Once you find an accountability partner, you might want to know what to do during your meeting time. There are many ways to conduct accountability, and here are just a few suggestions:

Open in prayer. Ask for God to speak, wipe out your pride, convict your heart, and help to you be completely honest.

Get caught up. It may have been a week or two since you had last met, so take some time to reconnect. Since this meeting should be a blessing and not a chore, enjoy getting caught up. Although you will be discussing some important life business, don't make it feel like a business meeting.

Ask about topics from the last meeting. Take some time to ask about the struggles and prayer requests from your previous encounter. Proverbs 27:17 says, "As iron sharpens iron, so one man sharpens another." This being the case, ask tough questions like these: How often and how focused was your time in the Bible? What types of sexual temptation challenged you this week? How did you fare with prayer requests? Any regrets this week? Any failures? Any victories? Be tough, be supportive, be a good listener, and be honest.

Discuss and implement strategies for improvement. Recognizing sin is a great step, confessing sin is very important as well. The next stride involves committing to a Godly solution to your struggles. Discuss what steps need to be taken to improve yourself in areas of struggle and schedule your strategies so that you follow through with them.

Introduce new prayer requests. Keep your accountability partner up to date on upcoming tests (academic and personal), challenges, and concerns.

Close in prayer. There is power in numbers, and Matt. 18:19-20 is proof of that. It says, "Again, I tell you that if two of you on earth agree about anything you ask for, it will be done for you by my Father in heaven. For where two or three come together in my name, there I am with them." Make sure to close in prayer.

Accountability will be an important piece of your foundation of faith. Ask God to provide you with an accountability partner, keep your eyes open for that person, avoid cross-gender accountability, and ask a trusted Christian leader for help when getting started. I am confident that you will find the benefits of getting an accountability partner worth the effort.

Keep Yourself Centered...Get a Mentor

The greatest challenge for most students is they feel as if they lack direction. What major should I pick? What classes should I choose? Where should I attend church? Relationships? Big Mac or double cheeseburger? To date or not to date? These are the questions of freshmen year.

There will be certain points during freshmen year (and beyond!) when you will have more questions than answers. It is in those times when it is important to have a person in your life who can share Biblically-based wisdom. The Bible says in Proverbs 1:4-5, "For giving prudence to the simple, knowledge and discretion to the young---let the wise listen and add to their learning, and let the discerning get guidance." What happens when we do this?

Steve, a senior who is majoring in engineering at Kansas University, has consistently searched for ways to improve his character. Because he was hungry for more maturity in his relationship with Jesus, Steve sought out two guys to be his spiritual mentors.

The two Godly men Steve picked were a few years older than he was and possessed spiritual qualities that Steve wanted to see in himself. These two men spent time teaching Steve about the character they had worked to attain in their Christian lives. They served as a resource when Steve had questions about a Bible passage, when he was going through a tough time, or when he was trying to figure out what God had in store for his future. I have watched this process in motion for the last two years, and now Steve is at a spiritual point far beyond where he was when the mentoring began.

We will pick out three aspects of the job description of a mentor from Steve's situation. First of all, his mentors were teachers. They spent time teaching Steve about the finer points of the Bible and how to live out his faith. Secondly, they were advisors. If Steve needed help with a given situation in life, they were there to counsel and advise him on what to do. Lastly, they held Steve accountable for spiritual growth. He experienced a tremendous amount of growth in his spiritual life because his two mentors consistently evaluated Steve's actions by God's standards. Mentors do many things. Most importantly, they teach, advise, and provide accountability.

What are some characteristics to look for in a good mentor?

- **Good mentors walk the talk.** They are people who live for God and serve Him in a way that you would like to emulate.

- **Good mentors are older than you.** They have been around the block, heard it all before, and have seen every trick in the book. Older people are wiser people, generally speaking. They don't have to be 40 years older than you, but they should be more than a few years your senior.

- **Good mentors are honest.** They tell you what you need to hear, not what you want to hear. In return, you can be honest with them. Honesty is a one of the most important elements of a good mentoring relationship.

- **Good mentors are trustworthy.** You can trust their advice, trust their confidentiality, and trust that they care for you.

- **A good mentor is available.** What difference does it make if someone has the best advice in the world for you if you never get a chance to pick their brain? Make sure they can meet with you every month. Availability is key.

Most churches and Christian groups on your campus have people who could serve as great mentors. Pray for God to put someone in your life that will serve as a mentor, and keep your eyes open. The top priorities when you first hit campus should be on finding a church home, getting plugged into a Christian group on campus, getting into a groove with quiet times, and setting up accountability. Once you have those things squared away, make sure to add a mentor during freshman year.

Given the confusion and chaos that college life can bring, it is easy to want to stray off the path of Truth just to get some answers. Having a mentor will help to keep you centered on the path until God's answers arrive.

Verse Memory: Your Best Weapon in the Daily Fight

Ever experience letdowns? Failures? Emotional hurts? Temptations? Unbearable circumstances? Doubt? Fear? Me too. The cool thing is that for every situation you could possibly go through in life, God has a verse for you to cling to. I believe we were given such a vast memory capacity (compared to other creatures on Earth) to be able to remember God's very words to us at the times when we most need them.

Psalm 119:11 says, "I have hidden your word in my heart, that I might not sin against you." From this passage we learn that a strong grip on God's word is the best way to prevent sin.

Jesus says in John 15:7, "If you remain in me and my words remain in you, ask whatever you wish, and it will be given to you." Have you ever needed comfort, peace, grace, encouragement, courage, resiliency, or any other emotion that is tough to come by when life has drawn its sword against you? Verse memory is the best way to instantaneously fight back during the worst of times, or even celebrate the best of times.

I confess that I've never had a firm grasp of verse memory. Although I can recall movie lines, song lyrics, and jokes with the best, I must admit that when it comes to Bible verse memory I am among the worst. My lack of discipline, not lack of ability, to commit God's words to memory has stung me many times recently. I've been in the midst of a sudden challenge and my perspective, actions, thoughts, or words will be far from God because my mind struggles to come up with His direction when I need it most. I hope you will add verse memory to the arsenal of your faith. I have paid dearly for not addressing verse memory sooner.

Having the promises and comfort of God's words close at heart is like getting a personal message from Him in a moment when the going gets tough. There are many great verse memory programs available in many churches, bookstores, and online, so get your hands on one today. Your life is guaranteed to be full of ups and downs. Commit five minutes a day to burning the Word into your mind and heart. Since everyday will be a battle, you'll need to know God's word to fight back.

Putting It All Together

Each of us has a deep thirst in our hearts that can only be quenched by interaction with God. Most students go through college constantly searching for something to meet the need of their parched heart. When students try to satisfy their thirst by pursuing relationships, alcohol, or achievement, it is like reaching for water and choking down sand. By pursuing God and taking root at the banks of His waters on campus, your thirst will be quenched beyond your wildest expectations.

God's Word, contained in the Bible, has furnished all necessary rules to direct our conduct.

Noah Webster

If I had learned education I would not have had time to learn anything else.

Cornelius Vanderbilt

Chapter 3

Preparing Spiritually for the Classroom

Oh the college classroom, how exhilarating or frustrating it can be! Some days you will be bored. Other times you will be excited, anxious, or relieved. And you will be tested...daily. Some of the tests will be academic, but most of them will be spiritual in nature. Most students experience times when they doubt their direction, lose motivation for studying, and wrestle with academic principles that don't fit Biblical truths. When, not if, these spiritual tests take place, you'll need to be ready. So before we walk through the ins and outs of a college semester (which we will do in the very next chapter), we will take time now to arm you with wisdom and encouragement for three of the spiritual tests you are bound to encounter in the college classroom.

The Bout with Doubt

It was the summer after my freshman year. I had just received a letter in the mail from the University of Minnesota stating that my application to the Carlson School of Management (U of M's elite business school) had been declined. "This has to be a mistake," I muttered in total shock. "I hit all their requirements. I was supposed to be a lock for the business school."

Instantly I was hit with questions. Should I switch colleges now? Is this God's way of saying that I'm not cut out for business? What type of job will I be able to get if I can't even get into the business school? Countless thoughts ran through my mind. I wasn't just disappointed. I was devastated. I was so certain that this was to be my next step. Then doubt began to creep in. Since I was wrong about my academic direction, where else in my life am I going wrong? Instead of running to the Bible to dig my head and heart into God's promises and His certainty, I foolishly sat back and allowed my mind to simulate a doubt-filled version of the rest of my life. Things looked bleak.

To finish the story, I was overcome with doubt until I closely studied Hebrews chapter eleven (what some call "The Hall of Faith"). I eventually wrote a letter of appeal to the business school. They set up a special list of academic requirements for me to meet during my sophomore year. I met those requirements, and was admitted into the Carlson School of Management as a junior. A year later I graduated with a degree in finance.

The truth is that, at some point, most students will have questions about their academic direction. Am I taking the right classes? Is this major right for me? Since I don't know what God wants me to do with my life yet, what should I do until I know? The trick, though, is to prevent those questions from transforming into doubts. How do we do that?

In the Christian life, we have questions when we have faith but lack answers. Questions are a good thing. However, we have doubt when we lack answers and lack faith. Matthew 21:21 states the following: "Jesus replied, 'I tell you the truth, if you have faith and do not doubt, not only can you do what was done to the fig tree, but also you can say to this mountain, "Go, throw yourself into the sea," and it will be done.'" In college, especially when it comes to academics, questions are inevitable. Doubt is optional. Faith is essential.

When questions arise and doubt appears to be on the horizon, please put these strategies into action:

Bury yourself in God's Word. The Bible is full of great promises, and all of them are true. Recently when I was very broken, I opened my Bible to Psalm 34:18 which says, "The LORD is close to the brokenhearted and saves those who are crushed in spirit." The safest place to be in times of trouble is in the Bible.

Spend time in prayer. When you have questions for God, talk to Him. And don't forget to listen for Him. Often times we think prayer to be a talking activity instead of a time to listen. I once heard a pastor preach on the importance of silence during prayer. He said, "What silence does is calm the mind and heart so that it is like the surface of a perfectly still lake. When we are this calm and silent in prayer, our hearts are more prepared for God's answers." Feel free to talk to God, but be ready to listen.

Trust the big picture. Time for a cliché: "Sometimes we're so close to the forest that we can't see the trees." Often times we stress out about the little things when we have no idea how they may impact, or even be a benefit to, the big picture. Proverbs 3:5-6 says, "Trust in the Lord with all your heart and lean not on your own understanding; in all your ways acknowledged him, and he will make your paths straight." We don't always understand what God is doing in our lives, and we're not supposed to. God has a better view of the big picture because He made the big picture! He knows what He's doing with you. Trust in that.

Chances are that you will have questions regarding your academic direction during college. At those times, bury yourself in the Bible, be sure to pray, and trust in the big picture. Apply your faith in such a way that you will easily defeat your bouts with doubt.

Academics: An Act of Worship

Have you ever performed poorly in a class due to a lack of interest? My entire finance curriculum at the University of Minnesota was a major yawner for me and my transcript served as proof. In non-finance courses my g.p.a. was a 3.8, yet I could only muster a 2.3 in finance classes. One simple truth eluded me as I put forth a lackluster effort and performance with my dreaded finance curriculum: studying is an act of worship. Let's explore this more closely.

There are approximately ten different words used in the original text of the Bible to describe worship. One of those is the Hebrew word *abad*, which means to "service or work for God." Colossians 3:23 says, "Whatever you do, work at it with all your heart, as working for the Lord, not for men." So when we are studying, no matter how boring it may be, we are actually doing work for God. He has entrusted us with a task, and our job is to carry it out to the best of our ability.

Most students have a hard time grasping the importance of completing a tiny homework assignment or finishing a boring chapter of a textbook. However, the Bible says in Luke 16:10a, "Whoever can be trusted with very little can also be trusted with much." Having diligence in the small things cultivates the work ethic required for the great tasks He has in store for us down the road. While the grade of that teeny one-page paper might not have long-term significance, the habit of hard work required to complete it is important.

Many students fall into the hardest academic trap of not taking seriously the task that God has given them. While most freshmen will struggle to keep motivated when their academic work draws more yawns than cheers, please keep in mind that studying is an act of worship.

Don't Believe Everything You Read

I was driving down the Minneapolis freeway on a recent crisp Tuesday, jostling with other drivers for the best lane position during the early morning rush. As I flipped around on the radio to catch a quick tune or two (my cd player is currently broken...praise God in ALL things!), I landed on a station that was broadcasting a sermon in which the pastor was speaking of an eye-opening experience in seminary.

As I recall, he was just getting into sharing a story about the first days of seminary, many years ago. One of his most memorable moments came during a conversation with one of his mentors. During the chat, the mentor said something to the effect of, "By the way, don't let seminary get in the way of your faith."

Some mentor, I thought. The pastor then went on to explain how so many people who seek education, be it in a Christian setting or otherwise, get so caught up in intellectual proof that matters of faith often fall to the wayside. The bottom line is this: just because an education may examine truth doesn't make it truthful.

Megan, who attends a small liberal arts college called Webster University, can vouch for the void of truth in her classes. "I took a religion class during my first year, thinking that it would be cool to study Jesus as part of a class. Well, the professor wasn't a Christian and most of the texts we read from weren't the Bible. I signed up for the course to help build my knowledge. What I got was a crash-course in spiritual self-defense."

You may have several classes on Biblical topics or none at all, depending on where you go to school and what you choose to study. Regardless of curriculum, the common mistake students make is that they will easily accept almost anything that is being taught to them. Like a sponge, they soak up everything that is spilled their way, storing it in as crucial information. Christian students need to sift what they are being taught through the filters of the Bible, allowing only the information consistent with God's word to permanently take root in their mind.

Your education may or may not have faith as a major part of your curriculum. Either way, be sure to measure what you are being taught with what the Bible teaches. In short, don't believe everything you read.

To Sum It Up...

Your time in the classroom will be full of tests. Some of them will academic, but most of them will be spiritual. It is common for students to have a bout with doubt, lose motivation for studying, and wrestle with academic principles that don't fit Biblical truths. As long as you prepare yourself for these tests, I am confident you will pass them with flying colors.

The great aim of education is not knowledge, but action.

Herbert Spencer

Chapter 4

What To Expect in the Classroom

Academics are perhaps the most common of common grounds in college. Regardless of the school you attend, your dating status, where you live, what church or Christian group you are plugged in with, or how you spend your time outside of the classroom, every student must spend time in the classroom. Virtually every student takes general curriculum classes and also courses specific to their major. More than likely, you will have interactions with professors and teaching assistants (we'll call them T.A.'s from now on). You will also participate in group projects, write papers, and study for finals.

In this chapter, I will walk you through academics from the first day of class through finals. Additionally, you will also be provided a segment of academic suggestions that come from some of the best students in the country. Armed with this knowledge, I believe you will be more confident when you hit the classroom.

Are You Ready for College Academics?

Do you feel ready for a rigorous college curriculum? If you are like most incoming freshmen, you are more than a little concerned about being able to make it through a college class. Why does college seem to be such a huge academic leap? You've probably been told that the classes are a lot harder. Perhaps you envision the classes to be much bigger. What's worse, there's never extra credit!

Believe it or not, most of the things you have been told about college are misconceptions. Yes, college is more challenging than high school. But classes are not that hard, most of the classes are quite small, and extra credit does exist. The class environment is different, and the scheduling is new. But just as God provided the tools David needed to overtake Goliath, you also have been equipped with tools that will help you when giant academic tasks stand before you. College is a natural progression from high school and is one you have been prepared for. Don't lose any sleep about whether or not you can "make the grade."

If you have been accepted to college, it is proof you are ready for that next step. No college would admit a student with the expectation that they would fail. Colleges want a high level of success from their students. When your application was under review by the institution of your choice, a panel of very intelligent people studied your high school performance. You were accepted because they felt that you were likely to succeed at their school. Most importantly, God deeply desires to be glorified by you in college. If His hand is on your life, the doors that were opened were by His doing.

If you graduated from 12th grade and have been accepted

into a college, you are ready for freshman year. Here are some tips from students like you that will help you succeed in your college classes. We'll start at the beginning of a semester…

Your Professors: Get to Know 'Em

A few years back the Minnesota Twins had a playoff caliber team, but they didn't have any big superstars. Their roster was filled with names no one knew and faces no one recognized. The marketing campaign that year was "Get to know 'em." Through a host of funny commercials, great promotions, and many exciting wins, we did.

In a similar way, your college classroom will be full of names you don't know and faces you won't recognize. Your job is to get to know 'em, with a special focus on developing rapport with your professors. This starts on the very first day of class.

The first day is mostly a breeze. Seventy-five percent of the time you will get a brief introduction from the instructor, go over the syllabus and academic expectations, and then arc let out of class early. Easy enough.

Laura, who just graduated with a degree in biology from Ohio State University, says it's important to introduce yourself to your instructor very early in the semester.

"Sometimes you want to introduce yourself on the first day, but only if the prof isn't getting swamped by a ton of students after class," she said. "If a lot of students are trying to meet the instructor, wait until the second or third class. Just meet them early, and show up for class.

"I got my 3.9 GPA by studying hard and making myself known. I always made sure that my instructor knew my name,

I always showed up for class, and I was consistent in going to office hours when I was lost on something. If you know the professor, you will have a better idea of what to expect on their tests and assignments. If a professor knows you, he or she will be more able to trace your progress and grade your effort and work quality accordingly."

Every instructor and T.A. is required to hold office hours. Instructors are usually thrilled when one of their students stops by because they rarely have students come in to ask questions. Even if you don't have an academic question, stop by to say hello once or twice.

Sometimes students don't know how to start a conversation with their instructors. Perhaps you could break the ice with something like this: "Did you envision yourself teaching this course at a college level when you were my age?" This question asks about academics and also about the instructor's personal life. From here you have an opportunity for a quality conversation about almost anything. And before you know it, your instructor will know your name and recognize you as a caring student.

It is important to develop a relationship in which your professors know your name and a little bit about you. Professors can serve as mentors or even as a part of your mission field. I knew of a student at the University of Minnesota who prayed for her professors and gave each one a Bible at the end of the semester. In addition, the quality of your work is bound to improve if you can talk with your instructor enough to get a good idea of what he or she is expecting from you.

Professors can play an important role in your life, and vice versa. Be a familiar face for your instructors. Get to know 'em.

Understand the Importance of the First Two Weeks

As a freshman in college I used to joke, "I'm going to start writing my book on procrastination today…unless the gym is open, or there's a good movie on tv, or I have an email I have to respond to." I was the master procrastinator during college (with exception of my former roommate Aaron, who would start looking for classes after the semester had already started!). Papers were always completed at the last minute, projects were never done early, and test preparation was usually an all-nighter. This habit of procrastination is dangerous. It starts early and catches on quickly. Here's how it begins.

College students usually misuse the first two weeks of a semester. During this time classes are just getting started and, for the most part, things are pretty easy. The material at the beginning of a course is typically review or is not tough to grasp for those new to the subject.

In addition to a light load at semester's beginning, students face another challenge: vacation withdrawal. More than likely, a new semester begins on the heels of a long vacation. Our minds are not necessarily in "school mode" when classes resume, and it can be a struggle to get back into the academic routine.

If you are coming off a long summer or winter vacation, here is an example of the type of vacation-withdrawal tactics your mind will be using against you during the first two weeks of class:

Instructor: "As we wrap up our first day, I want to encourage you to get going on the reading. Chapters 1 and 2 have been assigned for next time. Come prepared."

Vacation Mind: "Chapters 1 and 2 have been assigned for next time, but he didn't specifically say when "next time" would be. I could skip the next two class periods and read chapters 1 and 2 for next Thursday."

Instructor: "The first assignment is due in its entirety four weeks from today. The rough draft is due in two weeks. It's challenging, so I recommend getting started on it very soon. Feel free to come to my office hours with any questions you may have."

Vacation Mind: "I have a whole month until I have to do the assignment. The instructor thinks I should start in two weeks, roughly. Unless I feel challenged sometime very soon, there is no need to go to her office hours."

Instructor: "Attendance is not mandatory. However, most of the tested material is derived from the in-class discussions."

Vacation Mind: "Attendance is not mandatory."

You will be battling against your vacation mind now and again. Make sure it doesn't trick you into believing that the first two weeks are a continuation of your previous vacation.

Several of the students I interviewed made observations about the first few weeks of a semester. Professors assign a lot of chapters to read in the beginning class periods, but the readings are not very tough. Around week three the reading tends to slow down, and assignments begin to arrive. It's at this point that most students start playing catch-up. A majority of students, especially those new to the college game, sit back and take it easy until quizzes and homework start piling up.

The experts beg and plead with you to use the first two weeks wisely. Read the readings, attend class, and enjoy your progress while the pace is highly manageable. By getting the semester started off on the right foot, you set yourself up to be in a better position when things get tougher.

Those who slack the first few weeks are always trying to catch up. The first two weeks of any class are usually pretty easy. Take advantage of the situation, and avoid slacking off. Stop procrastination before it starts.

Study Buddies: The Difference Between A's and C's

Are you an independent studier or are you a study group type of person? If you prefer individual studying I have some bad news: college is full of group projects and group presentations. In addition, curriculum is so challenging at times that one mind can't always grasp each concept and group studying is required.

That being said, many students still mess up with their use of studying in groups. Here's some news: most people who study in groups do not do well on tests. Why is that? It's because they tend to use groups for the wrong reasons. The difference between an A and a C in college is how you use your study group.

Megan, a gifted scholar-athlete at the University of Minnesota, has a 3.98 GPA and is in an elite business school. One of the reasons she does so well is because she knows how to study effectively in groups. Here's what she does:

1) Reads through the chapters as they are assigned and reviews notes regularly.
2) Spends extra time on things she doesn't quite understand.
3) Visits a T.A. or her instructor at office hours to get help on things she didn't figure out on her own.
4) Studies in a group a night or two before the test to review the easy spots and tough parts alike.

Megan is no genius, but she works smart and doesn't count on learning all the information the night before a test. She also understands that groups are a great study aid, but only if you prepare on your own first.

Here are a few extra ideas from excellent students about studying in groups:

Learn by teaching. We often learn the best by teaching others. When a big test is on the way, divide up the chapters among group members. Have each person make a handout about the chapter and then take turns teaching one another. Don't do this the night before. Do it at least three days before the big test.

Study at a neutral location. It is very hard to study at someone's apartment, dorm room, or house. Get out to a coffee shop; get away from phones, email, and music, and just study.

Pick people who study the way you do. If you are very focused and like to study with few distractions, find people to work with who have a similar mind-set. If you like to get stuff done eventually and don't mind tangents, pick people who are up for off-topic conversations.

From a non-academic standpoint, studying in groups is tremendous for fellowship and evangelism. You'd be amazed how well you get to know your classmates after a few meetings outside of class. And if you use your study groups wisely, you'll certainly be better off academically as well.

How to Ace Your Exam: Go to the Review Session

What's the worst thing a student can do prior to a test? Not attend the review session! What's the second-worst thing a student can do prior to a test? Not prepare for a review session.

Review sessions can be either just like a practice exam where everyone gets a solid idea of what will be on the exam, or they can be a complete waste of time. What you make of them is completely up to you.

Instructors like to know that you are learning something. They want to know where you are genuinely stuck, not where you are clueless. If you really sat down and pored over a chapter and tried and tried to understand it but came up short, that is being genuinely stuck. If you come to the review session not having really studied anything yet and want to use the session as your first study effort, you are clueless. You need to investigate the material first.

Several students I interviewed recommended that I stress the importance of being prepared for a review session. Not all instructors are the same, but many will put questions on the test that were asked in the review session. In addition, your professors will give you an opportunity to try practice problems that will be on the test. The review session is a tool for both students and instructors. If you are well-prepared coming into the review session, your instructor is more likely to tip his or her hand and give you a good idea of what will be on your exam.

It is important to note that some instructors write the exams well before the review session. In any case, coming to the session prepared with questions may sway your instructor into guiding the review material toward what he or she has already written into the exam. Either way, attending review sessions is really important. Just make sure you prepare for them beforehand.

Get an Education About Your Education

About midway through your first semester it will be time to select classes for the next semester. Often it is unclear which classes are best to take, which ones fulfill the most requirements, and which ones are best to avoid. Seeing an advisor every semester and talking to older students about classes are the best ways to navigate through the system and find the best classes for you.

Matt, a junior at South Dakota State, is taking classes I wish I would have taken. He always seems to be pretty happy with his classes, his instructors, and the types of things he is studying. Regardless of the grades Matt earns in the classroom, he is successful academically because he is doing things that are fun for him. The reason he has picked all of the right classes is because he sees his advisor every semester to make sure he chooses classes that he will enjoy and that will count toward his major. Just make sure you prepare for it beforehand.

"It's important to talk to advisors every semester," he said. "You might get some insight about a class or two that really makes a difference. Besides, trying to pick the right classes can be incredibly tough when you don't know everything about what's offered. God calls us to be good stewards of our time, and it's easy to get lazy with course requirements and end up staying two or three extra years. Don't try to pick classes all on your own."

One of the reasons some students spend more than four years in college (and a lot more money, too!) is because they don't seek out advice and assistance when it comes to picking classes that will help them finish on time. Advisors are in place to help make the academic side of your life less worrisome. Most advisors are incredibly knowledgeable and helpful, but some are better than others. If you don't like your first advisor, get another one. It's important, though, to get some help in choosing your classes from people who know the school and curriculum better than you do. When I was applying for my degree during my senior year, I was able to fill out and sign my application with confidence because I knew I had fulfilled all the requirements necessary to graduate. There is no better feeling than knowing you have completed all that is required for such a large task.

There is one certainty about college: Tuition always increases. A semester next year will never cost less per credit than a semester this year. If you do not seek out an advisor for your course selections, you run the risk of not finishing college within four or five years. One of the worst consequences of finishing late is that the last couple of years could be significantly more expensive than your first years. Most students do not have an extra \$10,000 to \$20,000 set aside for a fifth or sixth year.

Being a good steward of our time and resources is what God requires of us. Getting an education about your education is a sure bet to help you graduate more swiftly and less expensively.

Get the Grade You Want

The purpose of a college class isn't to get a certain grade, it is to learn (and glorify God and be a witness, etc.). In every single interview, be it for an internship or for a full-time job, I have never been questioned about my grades. The focus has always been on my experiences and skill sets. So, what I'm telling you is that grades really aren't important.

Just kidding, they are important. This is because they measure more than just smarts. Grades measure attention to detail, desire, and persistence. Most students don't realize that getting the grade you want is not just about being smart.

Pay attention to detail. Have you ever found an error on a graded test or paper? It happens from time to time. Finals week is hectic in college for T.A.'s and professors because they have to grade a lot of work and get grades turned in. With all the grading going on, a grade or two is bound to be added up incorrectly. Since it is your grade, it is your job to take ownership of it and make sure that your grade is correct.

I once received a 55% on a final exam because the instructor forgot to add up the points from an entire section of the test. After I saw this oversight, I brought it to the attention of the professor. My grade on the final went up to a 90%, and my grade for the class went from a B to an A.

In total, I had five final grades changed in college due to such oversights.

From the first assignment to the last final, make sure your grades are accurate. Grading mistakes happen, and it's your job to catch them. Paying attention to detail will help your g.p.a.

Desire to be your best. God calls us to do our best in everything we do, for His glory. Therefore, in the classroom it is honoring to God to do well (with integrity, of course).

Ever wonder why people can hit a baseball, make a shot with a basketball, or hit the mark with a bow and arrow? We were created to hit targets. In order for us to do our best in the classroom, it is essential to set grade goals for us to hit. It's tough to hit a target if you don't have your eye on it. If you desire to be your best, set goals for the classroom.

Be persistent in academics. I once had a finance class where it took me forever to catch on to the material. I took the first test and failed it. I took the second test and got a D. I got a B+ on the final. And my grade for the course was a B.

Part of the reason I received a B instead of a lower grade was because I didn't give up. I was persistent in my pursuit of understanding the curriculum. In addition, towards the end of the semester I asked the instructor if I could retake the first test. Because of the extraordinary effort I had put in, he agreed. I ended up taking a test from a previous year and got an A on it. No doubt this helped my final grade considerably.

We are often reminded in the Bible that life won't always click when we'd like it to. That is why we are called to be persistent (in Luke 18:1-8 for example, the parable of the persistent widow). Don't let early academic setbacks get you down. Keep at the curriculum, get some help if need be, and see it through until you understand. When you receive your final grade, you'll be glad you persisted.

It is not easy to get the grade you want. Perhaps you've heard that extra credit is nonexistent and that instructors do not give extensions for late assignments. You could only assume that exams are the "make or break" opportunities of the semester. When you apply some attention to detail, a strong display of desire, and an attitude of persistence, the grading system is bound to work for you and not against you.

Free of Charge...

Here are some extra study tips from The Experts that I did not have time to expand on but did want to share with you.

- Take advantage of student tutoring services offered at your campus. It's free in many cases.

- Get general curriculum requirements squared away first.

- Find places to study that aren't the places you socialize or live.

- Set a GPA goal and make a plan to get there.

- Develop consistent study behavior.

- Know what your grade weights are. A one-credit class and a three-credit class do different things for your GPA.

- Passing or failing is on your shoulders. The professors will not hold your hand.

- Do the easy homework first to help you get rolling.

- Schedule study time.

- Take classes you are interested in. It will lead to your finding a major.

- The first exam is not always indicative of how you will do in the class.

- Group work always takes longer than you think.

- Group work is communication work.

- Have a mentor in your particular major to help you with classes, buying books, and learning the ropes.

- If you took a class in which you enjoyed how the instructor taught, look for more opportunities to take classes with that same instructor.

He may delay because it would not be safe to give us at once what we ask: we are not ready for it. To give ere we could truly receive, would be to destroy the very heart and hope of prayer, to cease to be our Father. The delay itself may work to bring us nearer to our help, to increase the desire, perfect the prayer, and ripen the receptive condition.

George Macdonald

Chapter 5

Will You Pass the Dating Test?

Many students fail the test within the first week. Others will fail it later on in freshman year. Some will ace the test four years in a row. This test is about dating. It's not just about your body, it's about your heart. It's about your intentions and your actions. Most importantly, it's about whether or not you put God above all others. The test has one yes/no question: Will you walk with purity in your college dating relationships?

THE Question of First Semester: Should I Date or Wait?

The first days of college life were very kind to an attractive guy like Ryan. So many new girls to meet, so little time. There were girls in class, girls in the residence halls, and girls everywhere in between. "Not bad for a small Christian college in Illinois," he thought to himself about Wheaton. "Not bad at all!" Some single guys in Ryan's shoes might consider this paradise. But not Ryan.

"It was really frustrating," he said when talking about the dating scene on campus. "All of my friends met girls right away and started dating. They disappeared for the first two or three months of freshman year, and then resurfaced when the relationship was over. While some students were quick to jump into dating, the rest of us focused on meeting as many friends as possible.

"As it turned out, the couples who chose to devote so much time to one person ended up missing out on a lot of the solid friendships that were being formed by everyone else around them." Ryan continued, "I was glad to wait on dating. It's really important to develop friendships with students of the same sex as you. For me, guy friends were my foundation of fellowship, and a dating relationship seemed to be something that would come after I had a solid foundation."

I must say that Ryan is a very solid Christian man, and I respect his opinion a lot. Did I follow his advice? No. Should you? Well, perhaps Emily's story can shed some light on that answer.

"I was really excited about coming to school," she said of her first year at Bethel College in MN. "I was on a sports team and was going to be meeting lots of strong Christian guys who were also athletes. The table was set for a relationship."

Emily started dating Chris, another freshman athlete. Within a few weeks, things were moving pretty quickly, and Emily thought that she had met her future husband. Unfortunately, she and her future husband broke up over Christmas of freshman year, and haven't really talked since.

"The relationship seemed like a really good idea at the

time. What happened, though, is that I ended up seeking my support from a guy instead of from God. After the fact, I realized that looking for a relationship right away isn't necessarily the smartest thing to do," said Emily. "Dating right away just seemed like a really attractive and easy option. But, the paths of least resistance are often those of least rewards. First-year relationships can take away from your experience. You are trying to get direction and learn more about yourself. It's hard to learn about yourself with someone attached to your hip."

So if the two students who were interviewed for this book recommend that you wait on dating, what did the other 241 students think? They vast majority agreed!

Allison, who attends Webster University in St. Louis, MO, is undeniably gorgeous. She did not date her first year despite countless offers from guys. "In the midst of change, it's vital to cling to the constancy of God, not the confusion of guys…or girls," Allison explains. "I changed so much during my first year of college. It took me awhile to figure out what my role was at school, and how God was going to grow my beauty on the inside, which is the one that lasts."

If you consider all of the areas of your life that are going through extreme changes during your first semester of freshman year (tougher academics, making new friends, being away from family, new involvement opportunities), it is quite possible that choosing to enter into a relationship can get in the way of addressing the challenges in your life and getting grounded with God. If you are in a dating relationship as you enter college, prayerfully consider laying the relationship down for awhile and being open to how God wants to teach you and grow you without having your heart tied to anyone else.

The first semester of college is incredibly tough. The best advice I heard time and again from current college students is this: come to college single, and wait a semester to date. Many students forget that their relationship with the Lord is the cake, and all other relationships are the icing...not the other way around. Assuming that marriage is what God desires for you, He will put that special someone in your life after He has prepared you for that privilege and responsibility. A semester dedicated to get grounded with God and acclimated with campus will only help that process along.

College Relationships: A Test in Protecting Your Heart

I love the Christmas season. When I was five, I used to get all excited about the presents. I didn't mind giving them (heck, it wasn't my money), but I was even more excited about receiving them. Those first times of getting presents really got me going. I can remember not being able to sleep at night because I was so excited.

Things are a little bit different now. I LOVE giving the gifts and still enjoy receiving them, not that Christmas is about the gifts anyway. But it's interesting to see how much the excitement gets watered down once you've been through a few rounds of Christmas. I used to run to the tree on Christmas morning. Now I passively stroll towards it, not nearly as excited as I used to be. It's almost as if I now take the exchange process for granted.

If you have been in a dating relationship, think back to that first dating relationship you were in. The excitement of the first kiss, the sweetness of the little gifts and phone calls and hugs and notes, the thrill of the quick wink of the eye or the shine of that big smile or the sound of his or her laugh or the…you get the point. How excited did that first relationship make you feel? It was like running to the Christmas tree when you were little, wasn't it?

Now think about your subsequent relationships. Envision yourself giving and receiving the emotional, physical, and spiritual gifts of a relationship time and time and time again. After awhile, that excitement level starts to fade. It's as if the gift of someone's heart is not as exciting as it used to be. Not only do you run the risk of taking another person's heart for granted, but your heart is also in danger of being taken for granted. Sad, isn't it?

You see, we were not intended to grow weary of giving our heart or receiving that of another. In order for us to fully appreciate the heart of our future spouse, we must keep the dating "gift exchanges" to a minimum so that we can still have the excitement to run like children to receive the heart that our spouse will someday give us as a gift.

Jesus calls us time and again in the books of the gospel to be like little children. In Matthew 19:14 Jesus says, "Let the little children come to me and do not hinder them, for the kingdom of heaven belongs to such as these." We are called to have faith like a child. Jesus said in Luke 18:17, "I tell you the truth, anyone who will not receive the kingdom of God like a little child will never enter it." We are called to take on the characteristics of children…to run to Him like children and to have the innocence of children. In Matthew 18:3 Jesus says, "I tell you the truth, unless you become like little children, you will never enter the kingdom of heaven." In the same way, God wants us to be like giddy little children when we give our heart to our spouse and receive theirs. In order to be child-like and Christ-like, we must understand that our heart is the ultimate gift that is not to be given away until the proper time.

Am I saying don't date in college? No. Meet people, hang out, and have a blast. What I am saying is treat your relationships in college more like Thanksgiving than Christmas. Be thankful for the person, pray for them, spend time with them, and eat with them. Just don't give them the gift of your heart, and don't take theirs.

The goal of college dating is to spend as little time as possible with someone who you won't be marrying. How do you know who you will marry and who you won't? I don't know. But most students give their heart away well before marriage is even a possibility. The bottom line is that many students, myself included, have the goal of dating backwards. Your job is not to look for someone to give your heart to, your job is to protect the gift until God delivers His season of courtship to you.

Here are some things you can do to protect your heart in college while spending time with the opposite sex:

1) **Keep time in check.** Arguably the greatest difference between high school dating and college dating is that time is on your side when you are on campus. You will have lots of time to spend with someone special. Mornings, afternoons, evenings, and late nights. It's important to understand that time does for a relationship what fertilizer does for a plant: helps it to grow. With the amount of free time in college, most relationships grow so fast it's as if they are on "time

steroids"! Keep time in check by spending it gradually, not all right away.

2) **Don't tempt.** Sometimes girls like to unbutton that extra button and guys like to wear the shirt that shows off the abs and arms. Perhaps it's that great back rub of yours that will awaken their body or the sweet words that will make their heart jump. Whether it's the clothes you wear, the way you initiate physical touch, or the things you say, please prayerfully consider acting in ways that will not tempt the heart or sexual urges of the other person. It's not as if you need to avoid showering or something. Rather, there is no need to showcase yourself. Don't make a conscious effort to awaken the heart and flesh of the guy or girl you are spending time with. Instead of leading their heart and mind away from purity, act in a way that will bring them closer to Christ.

3) **Share with caution.** Have you ever shared a fear, a dream, or a page from your past with someone? Sure you have. Have you ever wished you could "unshare" a dream, fear, or past event that you passed along to a member of the opposite sex? I'm willing to guess you have been there as well. When spending time with someone you like (or who likes you), it's vital to share yourself cautiously. You want your future husband or wife to know everything about you, right? Well, no one else should be equipped with enough information to finish even a close second place. As you unveil your character and emotional being to anyone you date, please keep in mind that your information is sacred. Share cautiously.

You only have one heart to give. In college, I pray you will spend more time protecting your heart than you will looking to give it away. God desires our joy and excitement to be like that of a child when we give our heart and receive that of our future husband or wife. By being conscious of the time you spend in dating, choosing not to tempt, and sharing your heart cautiously, you will be in position to both give and receive the best gift a man or woman could ever hope to open.

Sex: The Final Exam

We live in a sex-crazed society. Television, the internet, music, books, movies, and everyday conversations constantly sell sex and scream for our attention. All of the images and influences attempt to overtake us and drag us down into the standardless sexual revolution of today's world. Meanwhile, the calls for sexual purity from the Almighty God seem to be a faint whisper compared to the disturbing "noise" created by our culture.

The truth is that the constant barrage of society's sexual invitations are having a substantial effect on all teens, Christians included. Consider the following statistics from The Alan Guttmacher Institute: over 80% of students have sex before they are age 20, 10% of women ages 15-19 get pregnant each year, and 3 million teens acquire a sexually transmitted disease every twelve months. And despite how sex-driven our culture has become, people are surprised at the effect it is having on teens. That's like planting weeds and expecting roses. It is time to cultivate the garden of our heart and mind to follow God's call for our sexual purity.

I'm a big fan of the 4th of July. Every year, I try to make it to the fireworks celebration in downtown St. Louis, MO. They have a tremendous display right on the banks of the Mississippi, with the Gateway Arch as a scenic backdrop. The fireworks are awe inspiring, it's a great show.

It's amazing to me how many different explosions they can fit into one little firework. First is the comet-like trace of light that tails the path of the little rocket as it climbs into the sky. Next is the thunderous boom of the firework, simultaneous with the initial light display as if a star had just exploded. Then comes the changing colors from red to white to blue of the ever-expanding firework, and it looms larger and larger in the night sky. And finally, it will slowly fade away only to leave a trace cloud of smoke. Gotta love fireworks.

Every once in awhile, though, a dud is launched. It will climb only a few feet past the horizon, have a short and lack-luster explosion, followed by a brief anti-climactic display of a single color of light, and lastly a poof of smoke will designate its end. Duds don't happen very often, but when they do it is such a disappointment compared to the majestic experience of a true firework.

Ever wonder what separates a tremendous firework from a dud? Sequence. When a firework explodes correctly and in the right order, the intended and planned reactions happen in a way that promotes the best possible use of the elements, resulting in something truly glorious. With a dud, the spark of fire spreads too quickly to the wrong area of the firework, and this ruins the process, producing a much lesser effect.

I believe God designed sex like a firework. When a relationship catches fire in the right order and sex is saved for the marriage bed, it is a glorious combination of love, passion, and intimacy. However, if a relationship fires off in the wrong order and sex is had before or outside of marriage, the experience is a spiritual and emotional dud. Sadly, students too often settle for the dud. They never commit their relationship to God in a way that allows Him to control how the fire spreads in the relationship. Even in a case when a couple chooses marriage instead of continuing to settle for the dud, the beauty of the ensuing fireworks can be diminished by the haze of smoke left behind by the previous sexual duds.

So what steps can be taken to ensure that any relationship of yours is God-centered and dud-free? I believe the following is a must in today's sexually driven culture:

1. **Study purity**. It is always important to study what you want to become. If you desire to be happy, study happiness. If you desire integrity, leadership, or righteousness, study them. I pray that you will desire the joys of purity, so please study it. There are tremendous passages in the Bible that would make for a great Bible study (1 Thessalonians 4:3-8, Proverbs 4:24-27, 1 Corinthians 10:13, Ephesians 6:13). Secondary to God's Word, there are books such as *Passion for Purity* by Elizabeth Elliot, *Why True Love Waits* by Josh McDowell, *Every Young Man's Battle* by Stephen Arterburn & Fred Stoeker with Mike Yorkey, *When Good Men Are Tempted* by Bill Perkins, and *Not Even a Hint* by Joshua Harris. Additionally, courses on purity by Pastor Tommy Nelson, Dr. Douglas Weiss, and others are tremendous resources if you can get your hands on them. In studying purity, please keep in mind that it can't be done alone, or with the opposite sex. Grab a few Christians of your gender to join you in the study and find a mentor to guide the way.

2. **Set sexual boundaries**. Would you agree that there are certain places, topics of conversation, movies, television shows, magazines, and people that would lead you directly to

sexual sin if you indulged in them? Commit these "tripping points" to a list. Share them with someone who can hold you accountable to them. Most importantly, write down some escape strategies (Bible verse memory for example) for when Satan tempts you, because you will be tempted.

3. **Implement accountability**. Who is someone whose faith you admire? Who is someone that clearly has demonstrated sexual integrity? Who is someone you can be completely open with to share your struggles and success? Pray for and seek a person who you can meet with at least twice a month to openly discuss sexual purity.

4. **Take a serious look at the consequences**. A couple of years ago I found myself lost in sexual sin. In response to that, God laid it on my heart to feel the gravity of such a direction. I attended a benefit dinner for a teen pregnancy center and saw with my own eyes the devastation that comes with sexual impurity. This experience got my attention quickly. Premarital sex has serious consequences. I encourage you to take a serious look at the destruction of sexual immorality.

5. **Seek healing in your own life**. The bad news is that most of us haven't paid tremendous attention to how God wired our sexual fireworks. The good news is that Jesus died on the cross for each and every sin, sexual impurity included. It is important to confess our sexual sins to our accountability partner, repent (which in the original Greek means to "change one's mind"), and pray for God to heal our heart and mind to His standard of sexual purity. In addition, forgive yourself for past sexual mistakes. If God has forgiven you, then you also need to forgive yourself.

Although society tries to guide us into thinking that we are slaves to our animalistic sexual impulses, God's word states otherwise. The Bible states in 1 Corinthians 6:19-20, "Do you not know that your body is a temple of the Holy Spirit, who is in you, whom you have received from God? You are not your own; you were bought at a price. Therefore honor God with your body." The consequences of sexual sin are physically, emotionally, and spiritually costly. Due to the glorious experience God promises, I hope and pray that you will save the fireworks for marriage.

Passing the Test

In the Bible, God often tests people (see Isaiah 48, Psalm 17:3, 1 Chronicles 29:17...just to name a few). In college, you will be tested on your ability to spend quality time with the opposite sex in a way that glorifies God. The Bible has all the answers on how to pass this test, we've only introduced some of the questions here. If you can get grounded in God during your first semester, guard your heart as you spend time with your favorite guy or girl, and wait on sex until the fireworks of marriage arrive, you will be well on your way to having God say, "Well done, good and faithful servant."

The Bible has a word to describe 'SAFE' sex:
it's called marriage.

Gary Smalley

Your family and your love must be cultivated like a garden. Time, effort, and imagination must be summoned constantly to keep any relationship flourishing and growing.

Jim Rohn

Chapter 6

Family and Friends: How to Keep Up with those You've Left Behind

If you are like me, your childhood is flooded with memories that encompass an entire spectrum of emotions. Laughter, crying, embarrassment, excitement, frustration, anticipation. What really made those memories was not the way you felt, but who you felt them with.

As you enter college, the very people who have contributed to your lifetime of memories will suddenly be distanced from you. Most of your friends will be many miles away and your family will play less of a role in your day to day life than ever before. Changes are certain on the road ahead for the vast majority of your relationships. What will those changes do to your relationships? How can you stay connected to those you love? We will explore the gift God has in store for you and your loved ones as your relationships grow and change during college.

The Best Gift to Your Parents: Honoring Them

I can't remember how many times I heard Colossians 3:20 when I was growing up, "Obey your parents in everything." And most of the time, it was my parents sharing this verse with me. Life would've been a lot easier if the verse read, "Obey your parents in most things."

Many of the students I interviewed for this book shared a truth that I want to pass along: You will appreciate your parents so much more after college than you do at the beginning. They get wiser, kinder, and cooler throughout college. I believe that you will find life much easier during freshman year and beyond if you choose to communicate with your parents frequently, honor them with your actions, and respect them when in their presence.

Communicate with Your Parents Frequently

Sarah is a senior at Texas Christian University in Fort Worth, Texas, majoring in biology. "Prior to college, I wouldn't classify my relationship with my parents as very good," she said. "We didn't fight too much, but we certainly weren't best friends." She got closer to her parents while she was away as a freshman, and things have been great since.

"I called them a couple of times a week when school first started, mostly because they were really worried about me," Sarah continued. "After awhile, I was calling them because I liked talking to them, not because I was just checking in. Once I got in the habit of talking with them consistently, things started to click and my relationship with my parents improved drastically. Now I can talk with them about anything, and it's been fun getting to know them in a different way."

Notice that Sarah got in the habit of communicating with her parents. She wasn't necessarily wild about it at first, but once things got rolling she got a lot closer to them. The funny thing is that both you and your parents will benefit from frequent communication. You will get their excitement, sympathy, concern, and advice. They will get your energy, confusion, vulnerability, and need for help. Perhaps the best way to draw closer in any relationship is to invest time into it. Stay connected to your parents weekly. They are more of a blessing than you can imagine.

Honor Them with Your Actions

To be open with you, I was quite the "Curious George" as a freshman. I wanted to learn about Minneapolis, college life, parties, all-nighters, the whole bit. As curious as I was about my new life without direct parental boundaries, I was also true to my roots. I can recall walking home on Friday nights knowing that my parents had nothing to worry about. I had lived up to their expectations even when they weren't around to stop me from doing otherwise. This is not to say that I have never disappointed my parents or myself. Rather, while I was struggling to get properly planted in college, I held strong to the roots of my parents.

Just as the Bible calls us to be God-honoring with our actions, we are called to honor our parents. The best way to do that on a daily basis is to stick with the values they instilled in you. Proverbs 23: 22-25 says, "Listen to your father, who gave you life, and do not despise your mother when she is old. Buy the truth and do not sell it; get wisdom, discipline and understanding. The father of a righteous man has great joy; he who has a wise son delights in him. May your father and mother be glad; may she who gave you birth rejoice!"

It's human nature to wonder how it feels to walk off the cliff and free-fall into sin, and to wonder how bad it hurts to hit rock-bottom. However, it is God's nature inside of us that calls our hearts to walk in obedience with Him. Answer that call, and in turn you will be honoring your parents with your actions.

Be a Blessing When You are Home

Shannon, who attends St. Thomas University in St. Paul, MN, had this to say about going home for the first time during her freshman year: "Going home was great because of free laundry, home-cooked meals, and old times," she said. However, she had become more independent during her time at college and was not looking forward to being under her parents' reign again. "It was a huge adjustment going back home," she said. "I was used to running my own day, being independent, and following my own rules. My parents expected to be enforcers again, have me abide by their rules, and to consider them when planning my day. It was a huge adjustment."

Kinesha attends the University of Colorado-Boulder, and her parents live in nearby Denver. She sees them regularly and looks forward to going home. At the same time, adjusting to her parents is always a part of the game when she goes home for any extended period of time. In addition, she recognizes the need to respect her parents, adhere to their rules, and let them in on her college life.

"You will never be able to control all you do, all of your life," Kinesha said. "Coming home to your parents and honoring their rules is just good practice for what the rest of life is like."

Kinesha's visits home during college have been wonderful because of how she communicates with her parents when she's not home. She told me, "I call them a few times a week, let them know what's going on with me, and I ask them for advice. Parents know that no one is perfect. The hardest, but best thing I have ever done with them is tell them about my mistakes. They have more answers than I ever will. And that's why they are there—to help."

Do you feel as if your parents are willing to help you during difficult times? I understand that for some of you the thought of relying on your parents for advice is difficult to fathom. Some of you may come from a home where abuse or neglect has damaged your relationship with your parents. No matter the case, you deserve the opportunity to have a place you can call home. In addition, you deserve to have quality people in your life who are father and mother figures to you. If you do not have someone who you feel serves as a true parent in your life, consider taking some time to think about who could serve in that role for you.

More than likely, your parents want to be there for you when you are home and when you're not. I recommend opening up the lines of communication with them. Letting your parents in on your college life will enable them to see how you are growing and will help them be better parents for you. Going home can be great, but it may require some adjustments. The best way to prepare yourself and your parents for your time at home is by working on that relationship while you are at school.

How to Grow Your Relationship with Your Siblings

Do you have a sibling, or at least someone in your life that feels like a brother or sister to you? There is nothing like the bond between siblings. It is amazing how the differences, similarities, rivalries, stories and memories stack up to create a truly unique relationship. I have a sister who is twenty-six months older than me. Karen is in some ways my hero and greatest supporter. Yet, she is also the shadow that looms over me and the measuring stick by which I determine progress. I have an outstanding relationship with my sister and I love her dearly. Our relationship changed and improved during the college years.

I remember the first time I visited her on campus. I felt like the coolest kid in town; younger brother visiting his sister at college. We played pool, hung around campus, I met some of the girls on her floor in the residence hall. It was cool. The more time I spent with Karen, the more I respected her. She worked hard, achieved greatly, and was genuine with people along the way. I began to realize that I could learn a lot from her. And almost instinctively, she started giving me advice based upon what her life experience had taught her. It caused us to grow quite a bit, and I believe it will be a great tool in your sibling relationships as well.

If you have a sibling, the advice you give (if you are older) or the advice you receive (if you are younger) can really help to build your relationship. Speaking from the position of receiving advice, I know that I was truly blessed by the wisdom and the love behind it. Here's the scoop on giving or receiving sibling advice:

1) *It always comes with the best interest in mind.* Deep down, siblings really love each other. God created this special bond with a built-in "look out for each other" mentality. Therefore, even if the advice you are giving or receiving is not what you want to hear, you can still learn from it. Don't take advice as a personal knock or attack. Cherish it, because your brother or sister has your best interest in mind.

2) *The source doesn't have to be perfect.* In much of the advice my sister gave me, it was in regard to things she had done wrong that she wanted me to avoid. Occasionally she would pass along tips from what she did right. She was very balanced in passing along wisdom.

3) *Always Speak Up.* Sometimes, as a younger brother, I wished my sister would just keep her mouth shut and let me do my thing. She never did that. She was always putting in her two cents, for which I'm thankful. I don't believe we become used to taking correction by never hearing it. Advice is often very useful, so either speak up or listen up.

Advice can be a sore spot for some people. If you have a sibling, it can be an invaluable tool. If you are the oldest, kindly give advice where it is appropriate. If you are younger, kindly receive the wisdom being passed down to you. Either way, appreciate the reason behind it: love.

The New Role of Your Old Friends

I still remember my high school graduation ceremony like it was yesterday. As our principal delivered his message to the Parkway South High School senior class of 1997 he said, "Studies tell us that if you don't know the middle name of your friends in this room, you will not be in touch with them in six months. That piece of information alone can pretty well determine who you will stay friends with over time." Turns out he was right.

Fast forward to a few days before I left for college. My buddy Andrew called me over to his house and gave me a letter. It talked about how our friendship had come to be and how much it had meant to him. The last line of the letter read, "And by the way, my middle name is Reuben."

Almost seven years later, Andrew is one of my best friends and we still talk about once a week. He was a great friend during college, but not necessarily a close friend.

This is what can happen when a group of friends goes off to college. A few in the group will attend college together, perhaps room together, and constantly hang out together. College turns into high school part two, and those few folks bask in their little circle of friends. Then you have the friends who go to different colleges but try to constantly stay in touch. They email, chat on their cell, instant message, and are seemingly always connected. These folks may have a difficult time meeting new students because they are glued to their computer and cell phone.

Although it is important to spend some time investing in your long-distance friendships, it will be vitally important to focus most of your time on meeting new people. Ecclesiastes 4:9-10 says, "Two are better than one, because they have a good return for their work: If one falls down, his friend can help him up. But pity the man who falls and has no one to help him up." The bottom line is that you will need to have friends who can physically be there when you encounter tough times.

To put it in the perspective of a play or musical, the role

of old friends shifts from sort of a leading role to more of a supporting cast. They are still important and you couldn't get along without them. However, the amount of time that they "share the stage" with you is lessened. I'm not saying that you shouldn't talk to your old friends during college. To the contrary, as a supporting cast they can play a very important role:

Prayer partner-It's not a bad idea to talk with your old friends once a week in order to share prayer requests and get caught up a little bit. In fact, prayer is a great way to stay close.

Event coordinator-While it's not the best idea to go home every weekend, there will be times occasionally when a trip to see friends and family is a good idea. Please do keep in mind that you are at college to be at college. A good way to stay connected with friends is to coordinate with them for the holidays and various other trips home. High school homecoming, Thanksgiving, Christmas, or perhaps Arbor Day. Schedule some reunion events, but not too may.

Accountability-Chances are that it will take a little while to develop close friendships on campus. A good way to stay grounded in the Lord and connected with each other is to set up accountability with a long-time friend. While you might have an opportunity at some point to be honest, open, and vulnerable with your new friends, cultivating accountability with a old friend will be helpful as you settle in at college.

The sweetest thing about true friendship is that time and distance cannot undo years of memories and appreciation. Allow yourself and your old friends some room to make new friends. Stay in touch with your old friends, but be sure to let them play their new role as your supporting cast.

Keep Your Body at School and Your Heart at Home

To sum it up, college is a time when many of your core relationships will experience a lot of change. Develop strong lines of communication with your parents, lovingly provide and appreciatively receive sibling advice, and allow some relationship room so you can enjoy your new college journey with new friends. It is true that absence makes the heart grow fonder. Stay your course and stay on campus as much as possible those first few months, but tend to your heart by keeping in touch with home.

Blessed are those who can give without remembering and take without forgetting.

Elizabeth Bibesco

A baptism of holiness, a demonstration of godly living is the crying need of our day.

J.J. Packer

Chapter 7

Living Arrangements: Where to Live Out Your Faith

Do you believe that your home life has a powerful impact on how you live? Of course it does. The foods you eat, music you listen to, t.v. shows you watch, the quirks you have, and how you live out your faith are all deeply connected to the place you call home.

One of the realities that jumped out at me while conducting interviews was the importance of where you choose to live during college. Whether it is in a residence hall, with your parents, or in an apartment, your location sets up all other aspects of college life. Your living arrangement dictates a great deal with whom you spend your out-of-classroom time, what resources you have available to you, how you relate to other students, and how involved you become at college. It even determines where, what, and how well you eat. Deciding where to live is a big deal!

Timing is also important. You will most likely have four years to live as a college student. Four years is a long time. Some students are curious to live in a fraternity or sorority or to live off-campus. In this chapter we'll shed some light on where to live, when, and with whom.

Are Residence Halls Worth It?

It was unanimous. Not even a contest. When it comes to where the students recommend living freshman year, every single person pointed you in the same direction: the residence halls (rez halls for short)! The food demands an acquired taste, your personal space is challenged, many people don't operate on your time preferences, but it's an absolutely awesome place to be.

Dana spent her first year living at home while attending Utah State University in Logan, UT. She begged and pleaded her parents to let her live in the dorms, and finally got her wish granted for her sophomore year. If she could go back and do it again, she would do whatever it took to live in the rez halls freshman year.

"I really wish I would've left home and lived in the dorms for my first year," Dana said. "It's a priceless experience. Everyone is in the same boat, going through the same things at the same time. Being lost on campus, figuring out the phone system, turning that small room into the coolest place ever.

"Most importantly, I had a harder time finding Christian friends because I was never around outside of class to meet anybody. In addition, a lot of my friends at other colleges grew in their faith because they were forced to live out their beliefs. I really didn't experience those same spiritual challenges my freshman year. I missed out on that experience."

While living at home is definitely cheaper and is probably better for individual studying, you already have lots of experience doing that. Most of the real action during your college experience will happen at odd hours of the day and night, spending time as it is naturally available. There is no substitute for late-night movie-watching with new acquaintances in your hall and having that turn into an awesome bonding time.

Rachel, a sophomore who is studying marketing and accounting at the University of Texas in Austin, lived in the residence halls her freshman year and is back for a second year. She had the opportunity to live at home with her parents if she so chose, but even though she was really shy in high school, she picked the residence halls as her place to be.

"I made a conscious decision to be outgoing and meet people," she said. "I was really, really shy before college. By Thanksgiving of freshman year, my friends from high school were really surprised to see how much I had changed. You've got to grow, and the only way to do that is to bust out of your comfort zone. During meals, sit with anyone and everyone those first couple of months. Get a dry-erase board for your door so that people can leave messages. Get to know everyone on your floor by name." Rachel has maintained incredible connections with her high school friends, but has also really taken to the residence halls and become a new person in the process.

To me, the best part about living in the rez halls is that you are constantly available for God to use you to reach others. In Luke 10:2a Jesus says, "The harvest is plentiful, but the workers are few." That is the best description of a rez hall on any campus, Christian or secular. The most unique and rewarding experience of the rez halls is the opportunity to share Christ with your neighbors in need of a savior. The harvest is plentiful. Come and join in on some of the best work available for a college student.

According to the students I interviewed, if you have any way of pulling it off, definitely live in the rez halls. Don't settle for an off-campus apartment or a house with friends or even a fraternity or sorority in the beginning. It's gotta be the rez halls, and if you can't make that happen, living at home will help to save money so that you can get on campus as soon as possible. Now that you feel a little more excited about living on campus (which you should be), you can start pulling your friends together to start deciding on your roommate, right? Well…

Friends are NOT Good Roommates, Yet!

Are you headed to school with one of your friends? If so, perhaps you have the urge to live together during freshman year just to make it more fun. Avoid the urge! Being roommates is the kiss of death for many friendships. Here's why…

How good were you at driving the very first time you got behind the wheel? More than likely you were dangerous, at best! Why is that? It's not like you hadn't seen other people drive. You probably knew what to do, but it took some time to get used to doing it yourself.

The same thing applies to being a roommate. At the beginning of freshman year, most roommates are trying to figure out how to avoid interpersonal accidents. Being a college roommate is not just a different title, it's a different type of relationship. To this point you have had the titles of son/daughter, brother/sister, friend, perhaps boyfriend/girlfriend, but never college roommate. It really takes that first year to learn how to successfully live with someone outside of your family. Why ask one of your friends to be your crash-test dummy?

Of the more than 200 college students I interviewed for this book, all of them with the exception of one person, advised you to avoid rooming with your friends freshman year. Some people who lived with a friend their freshman year either:

1. Didn't meet many people because of their roommate/friend situation
2. Lost the friend over the course of the year, or
3. Ended up moving out before the year was over.

Taking your chances is a good thing for your first roommate. Trust me on this one, trust the students I interviewed, or trust Christy.

I have great respect for Christy's relationship with Jesus. She attended Indiana University, and, initially, she did not know many people on campus.

"I just trusted God with delivering a good roommate my freshman year," she said. "From what I saw in my dorm and what some of my friends went through, living with friends doesn't work out freshman year. I was blessed to room with someone who didn't know me before college because it forced me to really live out my faith.

"Deep down I wanted to be a bold Christian, but I didn't

know how to at first. As a freshman, I didn't know how to really communicate what it's like to have a relationship with God. So, I just tried to live it out."

"In addition," she continued, "I was exposed to so many new people because I wasn't constantly spending time with my roommate. It really helped to build a great circle of friends."

So far we've learned that the benefits of rooming with a total stranger these: they can serve as your crash test dummy, they can be a great witnessing opportunity for you, and they will afford you time to meets lots of new people. Let me suggest one more benefit: they will free you up to increase your time for ministry. If you don't feel obligated to spend lots of time with your roommate (which is the often the case when you room with friends!), you will have more time to wins souls for Jesus. Revelation 4:11 states, "You are worthy, our Lord and God, to receive glory and honor and power, for you created all things, and by your will they were created and have their being." Our reason for being on Earth is to fulfill the purposes of God, and a significant part of that calling is to be a witness, example, and testifier for God. Drawing from personal experience and that of Christian students whom God has used mightily, it's a lot easier to do God's work as a freshman on campus when your roommate is a new person in your life.

As for me, my freshman-year roommate and I had our differences. However, I wouldn't trade that experience for anything. He was a party-driven soccer player, I was a closet Christian. While I don't feel as if I made the most of my opportunities with Jim to be witness for Jesus, I firmly believe that I had more overall impact for God because my roommate wasn't a huge time commitment for me. As an added benefit,

I came back to campus as a sophomore more prepared to share my faith and live for the Lord.

Lastly, there is something about living with someone you don't really know that helps you learn how to really communicate. You learn tolerance, flexibility, and how to compromise in a way that couldn't otherwise be taught. It is instant interpersonal growth.

Your roommate freshman year is like a test-drive in preparation for the next few years of living with students. After you've mastered how to live with and tolerate someone new, then you will be more prepared to live with your friends. Trust in God to put a roommate in your life that you can learn from, witness to, and fellowship with.

Roommates and Living Situations after Freshman Year

The living arrangements after freshman year have a little different flavor to them. Most of the students I talked to did not have a preference about where to live during the second year of college (perhaps rez halls, perhaps not), but years three and four are time for houses and apartments for most students. You'll need roommates for that.

My last years of college were spent living with five other guys who I had met in a Bible study. We lived in this huge house a block from campus. We made dinner together once a week, had weekly prayer, and invited people over constantly for ministry-related things. Most importantly, there was a great deal of accountability in that house. If one roommate was putting their faith aside in some way, another roommate would call him on it. My faith grew leaps and bounds because of their presence in my life. I'm very thankful for those guys! Living with my close Christian brothers was the most fun I had during college.

An added benefit of living with multiple roommates during your time in college is that you really get to learn how to handle different personalities. My past two years of living in a house with my buddies has been awesome, and I've learned about how to better communicate with people. It's been fun, and I wouldn't trade it for anything.

One option to strongly consider is that of living in the residence halls as a community advisor/resident assistant. At the University of Minnesota we were called community advisors (C.A.'s), and we were provided free room and board and a small bi-weekly paycheck to live in the residence halls as a supervisor of sorts. It was hard work, but a total blast! And talk about a great opportunity to be a witness for Jesus and serve others! Look into it at some point in your college career.

Inside Evangelism: It's All Greek to Me!

The Greek system (fraternities and sororities) is a visible and lively segment of many campuses across the nation. Is it right for you? It really depends on your intentions.

When I was a freshman, I spent some time during my first semester at a few fraternity houses. In fact, I received bids to join two fraternities. The reasons I wanted to join? The guys at these frat houses were cool, had money, and had fun. Were I to join, it wouldn't be to serve as an example for Jesus. The reasons I decided not to join? I was the only Christian among them, their lifestyles weren't congruent with mine, and I felt that their bad habits would strongly influence me. I didn't feel as if my walk with the Lord was strong enough to withstand the types of attacks that commonly occur in a fraternity setting.

The truth is that the Greek system needs Christians…not just to visit them, but to live in them. That's what God did when He sent Jesus to us. Jesus came here to get his hands dirty for God, and we need students to rise up and do the same in fraternities and sororities. Jesus said in Matthew 9:12-13, "It is not the healthy who need a doctor, but the sick. But go and learn what this means: 'I desire mercy, not sacrifice.' For I have not come to call the righteous, but sinners."

God is going to call some of you to join a fraternity or sorority (not both, I'm certain!). Three of the Christian women I most respect at the University of Minnesota joined sororities. They joined as sophomores and juniors, not freshmen, and lived for a year or two at the sorority house. These women developed their faith so that it was strong enough to withstand the attacks of Greek life, joined their sorority for the purpose of evangelizing, and were used greatly by God to witness to those around them.

I would advise you to avoid joining a fraternity or sorority your freshman year…unless it is a Christian organization in the Greek system. It is wise to take at least a year to strengthen your faith. Furthermore, make sure your reasons for joining are God reasons, not goof reasons. And lastly, if it is your calling to be involved in the Greek system, live dangerously for Jesus and allow God to use you.

Closing Thoughts

The number one objective in picking a place to live during college is to put yourself in the best position to grow in your faith. For many students, the fellowship and ministry opportunities in the residence halls provides the best chance to step out of your comfort zone and grow closer to God.

It is indeed best to use freshman year as a "test-drive" experience with a roommate. There is plenty of time in the latter years of college to be roommates with your friends.

When it comes time to pick roommates, choose wisely. It is best in many cases to allow God to pick someone for you your first year. After that, prayerfully search for roommates who will provide the best accountability, spiritual encouragement, and an opportunities to minister to others.

If God calls you to the Greek system at some point in your college career, go! Just make sure your faith is strong enough to hold up to the surrounding temptations. Then...be bold.

I wish I could go through college again just to revisit the experience of living with so many cool people. Even though each and every second won't be perfect, you will learn much within the walls of your "college home".

If you are having difficulty loving or relating to an individual, take him to God. Bother the Lord with this person. Don't you be bothered with him - leave him at the throne.

Charles R. Swindoll

Prosperity knits a man to the World. He thinks he's "finding his place in it," while really it is finding its place in him.

C. S. Lewis

Chapter 3

Developing a Godly Perspective on Money

Almost all freshmen find themselves in a whole new financial demographic when they hit campus: poor college student. You know you're in college if you:

    a) See people on every corner asking you to sign up for a credit card.

    b) Act like a squirrel when you find a quarter, burying it away for your next laundry run.

    c) Eat ramen noodles like they're the last food on the planet.

    d) Write a check when purchasing an item that costs less than $2.

That's right, college is a whole new kind of poor. It's cool, though, because almost everybody is in the same boat.

Consider the following statistics: the average American will enter into debt at age 19 and will never climb out; the average amount of credit card debt for a college senior is over $4,000; and put one more glaring stat here. The real problem is that students typically come into college with poor money habits, and leave without ever figuring out how to manage money!

How can we rise above the mediocrity of the majority to blaze a financial trail worth following? The Bible is full of examples and instruction on how to properly manage money. The goal for this chapter is to demonstrate how to handle money during college in a way that glorifies God. Tough calling don't you think? Me too.

Bible-based Basics of Finances

Has your Mom or Dad ever given you money to go run an errand? In high school I was often sent to the grocery store to get a carton of milk or loaf of bread. Occasionally I'd be allowed to get something for myself like a candy bar or soda. Upon my return, though, the change always went back to my parents. After all, it was their money. To me it is interesting how, when God provides us with money to run the errands of life and afford a treat here and there, we aren't as inclined to give Him back any change. We think it's our money!

Christians seem to have money upside down. When it comes to God's money, either we don't know what to do or just don't do what we know. Either way, it's important to spend some time revisiting some Biblical principles that focus on tithing.

1. **All money belongs to God.** Consider Psalm 24:1, "The earth is the Lord's, and everything in it, the world, and all who

live in it." Everything on this planet is God's, including money. When it comes down to it, we really don't own anything. Rather, God has entrusted us with His resources. With that in mind…

2. **We are money managers for God.** The parable of the talents in Matthew 25:14-30 lays out this principle quite well. When God entrusts with money, our job is to manage it (spend it, give it, and grow it) in a way that glorifies God. According to the parable, when we manage God's money in a way that glorifies Him, we can expect to be entrusted with more. Matthew 25:21 states, "His master replied, 'Well done, good and faithful servant! You have been faithful with a few things; I will put you in charge of many things. Come and share your master's happiness!'" We are not only called to manage God's money, but manage it wisely.

3. **Money does not belong on a throne.** Many people pursue money as if it will increase their happiness, bring them a strong marriage, or heal sickness. Money does none of these things. God did create it to be a useful tool, but it is not to be worshipped. 1 Timothy 6:10 says, "For the love of money is the root of all evil." The most important part of that sentence is love, because money itself is not the root of all evil. In a world so focused on material possession and financial gain, it is easy to forget that the most important things in life are those that God gives us, not what money can buy us. There are segments of society that believe money is the deliverer of all good things. We must consistently remind ourselves that only God delivers good things, and money is just a thing that He delivers.

How easily it can be to forget that our money really isn't ours. In fact, we are just money managers for God. When we realize these truths, it is easier to see that money is not to be worshipped, for it cannot give us anything of eternal worth.

Truths About Tithing

I was 12 years old when I was first introduced to the concept of tithing. School had just let out for the summer, and I was doing my best to get a lawn mowing business started in my suburban St. Louis neighborhood. I was so excited one week to rake in a huge sum of money…$45! As I got ready for a rare Saturday evening church service that weekend, I was gleefully sharing the news with my mom of my recent financial success. Upon mentioning the huge amount of money I had earned that week, my mom stated, "You need to give $4.50 to the offering plate at church tonight. God's provided those opportunities to make money. Now you need to be give back part of what He gave you." Welcome to the concept of tithing.

I was mad! How does one make money by giving it away? At any rate, I did as I was told and parted with 10% of my week's earnings. Something interesting happened when I got home from church that night. Upon reaching the driveway of our house, I saw one of our neighbors walking toward our door. As it turns out, she was going out of town for three weeks and was hoping I would mow her lawn while she was away. She gave me $45 that night as payment for the upcoming lawn work. I've been adamant about tithing ever since.

So what exactly is tithing? The word tithe means tenth. To tithe means to offer God a tenth of what God gave you.

With that definition in place, let's examine some three tithing truths.

1. **It's about value, not amount.** I felt for a long time that I would have to tithe a lot of money in order for it to make a difference. In the book of Mark, there is a story about a poor widow who gives a fraction of a penny. Mark 12: 43-44 states, "Calling his disciples to him, Jesus said, 'I tell you the truth, this poor woman has put more into the treasury than all others. They all gave out of their wealth; but she, out of her poverty, put in everything---all she had to live on.'" In this case, giving less than a penny was worth a lot because it is all the woman had to give. The value of your tithe has nothing to do with the amount you give.

2. **We are called to give in full.** Christians, on average, give 2% of their income. How does a 2% tithe measure up to God's standard of at least 10%? Malachi 3:9-10 says, "You are under a curse --- the whole nation of you---because you are robbing me. Bring the whole tithe into the storehouse, that there may be food in my house. Test me in this," says the LORD Almighty, "and see if I will not throw open the floodgates of heaven and poor out so much blessing that you will not have room enough for it." It's also important to notice in this passage that God promises to respond to our faithful tithing. However, God's response is not so that we can just have more for ourselves. The passage says that we will "not have room enough for it." If we are provided with added financial provision, it will be for the purpose of additional giving. Always make sure to give in full.

3. **Tithing should be a sacrifice sometimes.** The scripture

in Mark 12:43-44 also demonstrates that tithing is not just about giving your excess wealth, it's about giving all you can. This poor widow offered God all she could possibly give. Tithing is more significant when we give beyond what is financially comfortable. With all due respect to budgets and bills, God loves when we give in a way that causes us to rely more on Him. Don't be afraid to give when finances are tight. God delights in that sacrifice.

With these truths in mind, I encourage you to take tithing seriously. Giving to God is an act of worship. When you realize the how valuable your tithe is in the eyes of the Lord, tithe in full, and even allow yourself to give to the point of sacrifice, you will be amazed at how God will respond to your financial faithfulness.

Two Things to Do with Credit Cards: Jack and Squat

Free t-shirts! Free cd's! Free highliters! It's too good to be true. All I have to do is fill out this harmless credit card form and the free stuff is all mine? Oh baby, where do I sign?

I found myself thinking this way about credit cards on my first day of school. There is a part of our make-up that wants to get caught up in materials. It's the desire to acquire! And it seems easy, I just sign up for this credit card, get the free stuff, and then cancel the account when the card comes in the mail. What I didn't know is that signing up for credit cards and then not using them can be bad for one's credit. If you sign up for a credit card without the intention of using it, you might be putting yourself into a dilemma. One of the following two things could happen:

1) You close the account immediately and put a blemish on your credit report, or

2) You misuse the card, spend yourself into debt, and put a blemish on your credit report.

Avoid the trouble! Your credit will be important later on when you want to buy a house or a car. Most freshmen should steer clear of credit cards their first year. So what if you get a free t-shirt. Do you know how many people will have that same shirt? Are you ever really going to use the free stuff credit cards companies give you? Why do you think it's free?

No matter what the incentive, credit cards are misused all too often. Of the people I interviewed who had credit cards as freshman, most of them had credit card problems. I have friends who are still paying off credit card debt from three years ago at outrageous interest rates.

Gabriel, an athlete who just graduated from Black Hills State, has spent the last few years trying to recover from his freshman year credit card debt. He spent unwisely and then committed the cardinal sin of them all: paid the minimum possible payment! Man, did the interest add up on him. He's so poor that, for this interview, he had to call collect. Actually that's not true, but he is still spending his time and money trying to play financial catch-up from his freshman year.

Not many students seem to know this, but not making a full payment on a credit card bill has two major ramifications. First of all, the interest charged to you for not paying in full is outrageous. Credit card companies make their money on interest. And once again, not paying in full is bad for your credit. Having bad credit is like having a criminal record.

Banks and loan officers will be on the lookout for you. Purchasing a house is more expensive when you have bad credit because the interest rate on your loan will be high.

Some people sign up for a credit card with a "specific need" mentality. They think, "I'll buy the last few outfits I need to polish off my look and then I'll never use it again. Well, maybe I'll use it for gas, or pizza, or cd's, or snacks, or stuff at Target. Oh man, I've got a lot of credit card needs!"

I'm not going to spend this whole section slamming credit cards. They can provide a good opportunity to build credit. They can help people track expenses because all of your transactions show up on the bill. They also have some packaged incentives on airline tickets and rental cars that can be helpful. Despite all the possible benefits, using credit cards early in college can be a big gamble.

Here's the problem with credit cards and freshmen: Some of us are accustomed to having mom and dad buy us things whenever we need them. Most high school students take for granted the snacks here and there, pizza for dinner, and an item or two from the store whenever needed. College rolls around and we have this habit of spending whenever the situation calls for it. The difference now is that our parents probably aren't footing the bill! We pamper ourselves without realizing how much money we are spending. It's amazing how quickly $500-$1000 creeps up on your monthly bill.

I just finished my degree in finance and I interviewed other finance and business students who are very financially aware. I also interviewed students in the arts and people who are seeking degrees in various sciences. No matter what they were studying, anyone with solid common sense said it was important to develop a good financial foundation and learn how to conquer the spending bug. With a credit card you can spend at will. Without one, you can't spend what you don't have.

If anything, go nuts and get a debit card. You can't overspend by much with a debit card because the money is taken straight from your bank account right at the time you use it.

God calls us to be good stewards of money. In this case that means we must apply one of the most fundamental (and most often ignored!) financial truths: Don't spend what you don't have. Everyone I talked to suggested that every freshman should consider staying away from credit cards. Get used to your new level of financial independence. Get a credit card later on in college and begin to build credit at that time. You deserve to enjoy freshman year without burying yourself in debt.

Seek God's Provision through Grants and Scholarships

Beth is a married college student. She now lives off-campus with her new husband. When I interviewed Beth, she definitely had something to say about scholarships.

"There are so many scholarships out there," she said. "As a freshman, I had no idea that there were scholarships for virtually every type of situation. I applied for some, but wish I would've applied for more. For some reason I just didn't want to write the essays and meet all those requirements. It might take ten hours of work to get everything prepared for one scholarship, but if it's a $2000 scholarship, that's like making $200 an hour.

"I know of so many students who are on their knees asking God for financial provision," Beth continued. "They don't actively seek scholarship and grant avenues that God could easily use to bless them. It's almost as if most Christian students are waiting for God to bless them with the holy lottery. Freshmen really need to think about pursuing grant and scholarship opportunities throughout college."

None of the students I interviewed (except those at college on full scholarships) felt as if they had put their all into the scholarship search. I wish I had spent more time getting free money. I have very little debt coming out of school, but I could have wiped out my debt with one or two scholarships. Most students think scholarships are for incoming freshmen. In actuality, there are thousands of scholarships out there for every type of college, every single field of study, and almost every single special case. But scholarship money doesn't come knocking on your door. You have to seek it.

Consider what Jesus says in Matthew 7:7-8: "Ask and it will be given to you; seek and you will find; knock and the door will be opened to you. For everyone who asks receives; he who seeks finds; and to him who knocks, the door will be opened."

I don't believe this verse wants us to consider God to be some sort of genie in a bottle. Rather, Jesus is promising us that we will be given direction and wisdom when we ask and seek. It's great to have faith that God will provide. It's also a good idea to put some action behind that faith and seek out avenues that God may want to use to provide financial assistance. To help you with finances, here are a few scholarship search tips:

1. _Ask_-Pray earnestly for God to give you the eyes to see possible avenues He may want to use to bless you. And, it doesn't hurt to pray with a specific amount of money in mind. Our God is detailed. If you need proof of that, notice the detail and specificity in the last four chapters of Exodus through the book of Numbers.

2. _Put potential avenues on paper_-Write down your interests, skills, quirks, traits (perhaps you are left-handed, have a unique bloodline, or are a twin), and family network (possibly you are linked to a war veteran, teacher, or loved-one with a disability).

3. _Seek out resources_-Each college has a financial aid center. Every area of study has national contests for scholarship money. Every state has organizations that help students find money. Seek out those resources!

A Part-time Job: A Must for Most

Liz attends Taylor University in Indiana, is an incredible student, and is majoring in English. When her interview began, the first thing she said was, "Tell freshmen to get a job, on campus if possible. There's time to work." Liz is most certainly an overachiever and has a lot of things going for her. Having a job fits her well, as it would for many of you as you begin college.

When it comes to having a job at school, there are plenty of positives:

1. It is helpful in developing time management,
2. A place of work is a great place to develop work ethic,

3. You can have some money to live on, tithe with, and save for paying tuition,

4. A job allows you to build skills and keeps you from wasting your time and your abilities, and most importantly,

5. A job provides a great place to share Jesus with others and experience fellowship.

I can certainly understand the philosophy of wanting to focus on studying and not wanting work to interfere with that. A strong grade-point average and a degree will usually be able to out-earn any college job over the long haul. However, anything you can do to earn some money and reduce your expenses or loans will be of enormous benefit to you. Most students never have much money because they choose not to work. My expert panel highly agrees that getting a job, on campus if possible, is a great way to help win the war on debt. Be a good steward of your time, your money, and your faith…get a part-time job.

Pursue a Godly Perspective on Money

We deal with money on a daily basis, and yet very few people actually know how it can work for them or against them. College students seem to be especially oblivious to money matters, which is tremendously alarming because it is during the college years that most "make or break" financial decisions and habits are made.

It is funny to think that what we have isn't really ours. Everything in this universe is God's. What is currently in our possession has been entrusted to us, but it isn't ours. Any time we gain or lose money, it should be with the realization that it's not ours anyway. Romans 11:36 states, "For from him and through him and to him are all things. To him be the glory forever! Amen." And as quickly as it comes, it can just as easily be taken away. That's why Jesus calls us to store up treasure in heaven and not on earth (Matthew 6:19-24).

The Bible tells us that our money is not really ours (Proverbs 24:1), warns us that we can't serve both God and money (Matthew 6:24), and encourages us not to worry about money (Matthew 6:25-27). We are told that the love of money is the root of all evil (1 Timothy 6:10) and are instructed to not be greedy for money, but eager to serve (1 Peter 5:2). The only topic the Bible mentions more than money is love. With as much focus as the Bible commits to the subject of money, we need to spend some time learning how God wants us to handle something that, although it is important in daily life, we certainly can't take with us into eternity.

A Few Parting Financial Thoughts

College is expensive; there's no doubt about it. Most of you will finish college and have some debt to pay off afterward. How much debt you have is completely up to you. Establish good money habits. Many great books and tapes can quickly teach you how to conceptualize money in a useful way. I've pursued a financial education through two avenues: 1) conversations with wealthy men and women of God, and 2) books anyone can find in a bookstore. Learning how to use money in college will help you to navigate around the pitfalls of unnecessary debt. In addition, you can develop ways to pay off debt quickly and have money and interest work for you. Whether you spend your college years developing wise money habits or cultivating poor habits is up to you. Most likely, though, it will be the difference between having a little bit or an overwhelming amount of debt after college.

The purpose of tithing is to secure not the tithe but the tither, not the gift but the giver, not the possession but the possessor, not your money but you for God.

Anonymous

You only live once, but if you work it right,
once is enough.

Joe Lewis

Chapter 9

The Once-in-a-Lifetime Experiences of College

Some things about college are universal. College is going to cost someone (maybe not you or your parents, but someone) a lot of money. Food in the residence halls is going to get old. If you stay up late enough at night, you are bound to find *Boy Meets World* reruns. And… college is absolutely awesome, unless you keep yourself from getting involved.

At every school there are countless ways to immerse yourself—intramurals, fraternities, sororities, sporting events, academic clubs, social clubs, Christian groups, special-interest groups, and support groups. Taking ownership and feeling as if you belong are essential aspects of your college experience. You don't just go to college, live at a college, or study at a college. You are college! It is the collective energy from each and every person on your campus that will determine what type of environment your school offers.

College is a once-in-a-lifetime deal with once-in-a-lifetime experiences. Getting involved is not just about finding organizations to help you spend your time. It is diving into the right things for you that will glorify God and make your experience well worth the price of admission.

So, free up your mind and consider some advice on a few once-in-a-lifetime opportunities our panel of students know a lot about.

Get Up and Go

Which is better, going to a game or watching it on tv? Which is better, attending a concert or reading about it the next day in the newspaper? Which is better, supporting your friend in person on a college stage or just hearing about your friend's performance?

According to many of the students I interviewed, you as a freshman are either one of three people. Either you

    a) Know exactly what you want to jump into and can't wait to get started,

    b) Have some idea of how you'd like to spend your extra time but don't know of a student group that does what you want to do, or

    c) Are tentative about commitment when it comes to getting involved in college and don't know where to start.

Or you could be a combination of any one of these descriptions. No matter how you feel about getting involved, the first step is the same for freshmen. Get up and go!

I must admit that I was one of the least involved students for most of my college career. I attended one football game during my first three years of college. I went to the homecoming football game freshman year when the Gophers were severely beaten by Ohio State. All of my friends were going to the games my sophomore and junior years, and finally I decided to get season tickets my senior year. It was a blast going to the games! Even though I saw some really good games, I ended up enjoying being around the people more so than watching the game. The environment, experience, and electricity can't be beat—regardless of the result of the game.

Several students recommend that you try going to an event even if you don't think you will necessarily enjoy it. All you have to do is watch, which is really easy. And you'd be surprised how much fun you might "accidentally" have. But please, by all means, don't be like me and miss out on events during your college career. Go to the games, go to the plays, and go to the musicals. These events are a great place to meet people, to feel connected, to develop school spirit, and to minister to others.

Far and Away: The Best Involvement Ever

Do you want to be a missionary? Would you simply like to learn about other parts of God's creation? The best possible involvement opportunity is simply to distance yourself from your campus and your college. By getting away from everything, you have an opportunity to develop a deeper appreciation for your school environment and to feel excited about wanting to get plugged in. Therefore, the very best thing to do in college is to go far and away to develop a taste and an admiration for your world: Study abroad!

If I could go through college again, I would make sure to study abroad. Every single person I interviewed who talked about this opportunity had positive things to say about the experience. Here's what you need to know about studying abroad:

1. *You Don't Have to be a Foreign Language Expert*

One of the main reasons I never pursued an overseas experience is because I thought I had to be taking French if I wanted to go to France. Not so! None of the students I talked to had taken classes in the foreign language of the country they were visiting. It's a good idea to at least learn the basics so that you can find a restroom and buy a meal, but speaking the language fluently is not a requirement.

2. *Go Early and Go Alone*

When's the best time to go? Spring semester of your sophomore year or fall semester of your junior year are the best bets. If you go too early you may not get all of your required curriculum squared away, and then you run the risk of falling behind academically. If you go too late, there's the possibility of missing out on interviews for internships or jobs during junior or senior year. It's best to go in the middle of your college career, if possible.

In addition, no student should experience this adventure with a friend. Plenty of students from all across the nation will be on your trip. If you travel with a friend, you miss out on appreciating the people around you. Also, this is a great time to depend on God alone. Why would you want to ruin that for you and a friend? Another reason it is best to go alone is because you will...

3. Develop a Heart for the Lost World

Ben studied abroad in Germany for a semester. He also traveled to several countries, including France. "What struck me about most of Europe," explained Ben, "is that few people over there really believe in God or talk about faith. It's as if faith is a dead issue. You see all the wonderful churches that were built so long ago, and you begin to wonder how those churches turned into just a building. It broke my heart, but also got me hooked on wanting to be used by God to bring faith back to the lost of the world."

It's funny how experience and perspective work together. I used to think St. Louis was cold in the winter until I came to Minneapolis for college and learned what cold really meant. I also thought the hill in my back yard was pretty big until I skied in the Rockies. In the same way, students who studied abroad said they gained a whole new perspective and appreciation for America, the country they visited, cultural differences, traditions, mankind in general, and the world. This opportunity is unparalleled in your college experience.

Studying abroad may be expensive, but scholarship opportunities and loans are available. If money is the only issue, please make it a non-issue. This experience is priceless!

Politics, Service, and Professional Groups on Campus

One common criticism of Christians is that we like to stick very closely to a handful of Christian causes. We keep our Christian mentalities and Christian resources to our Christian groups, and then we lash out our Christian judgment to every group that is not following God. While I am exaggerating a little bit, there is certainly something to be said for jumping right into a cause on campus that has no direct ties to a church or Christian group. The disciples didn't spread the gospel by avoiding other people, they spent time with them. Several students and Christian group staff members recommended that you consider taking part in a non-Christian cause for the sole purpose of being a light in the darkness.

There's no doubt about it, college is a hot-bed of seemingly unlimited causes: cancer research, politics, services for the underprivileged, environmental protection, disability services. The list is almost endless, which is a good thing. Pick a group and go for it.

I must say that Eric is right in the middle of things with Habitat for Humanity at the University of Minnesota. He plays a large role in getting funding together and getting projects rolling. Being the great man of God that he is, I'm glad he's in the position he's in. He is at the top of an organization at his campus, and is able to shine his light for Jesus to everyone. He doesn't preach to the students he works with or anonymously put fliers around their work sites. Instead, he works side by side with students who are in dire need of spiritual direction. When they stop and notice how God's presence in Eric's life directs his steps, they ask him about it. And the thing is that Eric isn't anything out of the ordinary, he's just available. There is something invaluable about being available when it comes to doing God's work.

Please don't believe that you are expected to bury yourself in eighteen campus causes just so you can be amongst the hurting hearts of the world. Instead, prayerfully pick one. You don't have to be the president of the club or any part of their leadership, you just have to be there. Be active in a cause on campus. God doesn't want us to shut ourselves out from the world.

Important Tips for Getting Involved

What you choose to get involved in is completely up to you. My expert panel recommended considering the following when picking an outlet for your energy:

- Stay true to your convictions when joining a Christian or non-Christian club.
- Get involved in a group because it interests you, not because it interests your friends.
- Choose something to do that is non-academic. You're in class enough as it is.
- Place some energy into something outside the college community, such as a hospital, park, museum, or children's center.
- Go to a few meetings and consider joining a club or two. It's the best way to meet quality people.
- Have one activity in which you have great depth of involvement all the way through college.
- Treat college groups like Old Country Buffet—go around a few times and try everything before you sink your teeth into one thing.

Any activity that takes up your time should include the following: a chance to get plugged in, an opportunity to get something out of it, and a time to give back. If you consider these things when pursuing an activity on campus, you will most definitely be able to narrow down some options and find opportunities suited for who you are and what you are passionate about.

To Wrap It Up

Regardless of how outgoing you are, no matter how academic-heavy your schedule, despite any reservations you may have, the most important element of your college career is going to be your activities outside the classroom. Many of your best college memories will come from your involvement in campus life. Your activities will also be a place where you can take a break and be energized for classes and other stressful parts of your life.

As if getting plugged in didn't have its own rewards, your involvement in activities during college can also be a powerful tool on your resume. Businesses are always looking to hire people who are well-rounded and have more to show in their college experience than just a strong GPA.

I have never heard any college student say, "Don't get involved in anything outside the classroom. It's a complete waste of time." Do you wonder what's going to happen by getting plugged in? You will be trying new things, meeting new people, learning about life, helping in the community, and making a difference on your campus. Your classroom knowledge alone will not take you where you want to go in life. The growth and life experience you gain by taking part in the once-in-a-lifetimes on your campus will complement your academic endeavors and be a truly magical piece of what makes your college life and the rest of your life electric. You have one life and one shot at college. Why not explore what once-in-a-lifetime experiences God has in store for you?

There are two ways to live your life. One is as though nothing is a miracle. The other is as though everything is a miracle.

Albert Einstein

The progress of mankind has always depended upon those who, seemingly isolated and powerless in their own day, have seen their vision and remained true to it. In the darkening corridors of time, they preserved integral their vision of the daylight at the end. This is a matter not of calculation but of faith. Our work may be small and its results invisible to us. But we may rest assured it will come to fruition in God's good time.

John Ferguson, *The Enthronement of Love*

Chapter 10

Forward Thinking: Finding Passion, Picking Majors, and Preparing for a Career

When it comes to making plans and building a future, the world offers us contradicting advice. We are told that "those who fail to plan, plan to fail." Yet we also hear that "the best laid plans often go awry." And even though what is planned and what actually occurs are often times different, college students are asked to confidently map out a future. Pick a college, choose a major, select internships related to that major, and settle on a career that is connected to your degree. You are asked to start planning out your life the day you hit campus.

With so much at stake so soon, perhaps it will be helpful to provide some insight into exploring passions, picking a major, serving for a summer, and lining up work during college. We'll start by trying to get some Godly perspective on how we should view our plans.

Figuring Out the Puzzle

How good are you at putting together puzzles? I'm not very good at it because I'm not that patient with them. I usually end up jamming in a piece or two that doesn't really fit right. I suppose I do this because I want to feel like I have all the pieces in place. In fact, a lot of people do that in life. They will choose a major, career, or spouse just to have the pieces in place, even though the pieces might not actually fit.

What many people haven't figured out is that we are not supposed to put the puzzle of our life together. That's God's job. It's His puzzle. In fact, we don't even have our own puzzle. We're a piece in His puzzle. So instead of wasting time trying to figure out "where all the pieces go", we would be much better off asking God how we fit into His puzzle.

If you are wondering why so many of ours plans fail, it's often because we are puzzle pieces trying to be the puzzle maker. How about when things do work out? When great men and women of God have plans that succeed, it is because God did the planning. In these cases, He will plug a person into a situation where they are a good fit. When you are where God wants you to be, all the pieces tend to come together around you.

To put the analogy aside for a moment and focus squarely on the truth behind it, our plans fail because we create them. Proverbs 16:9 says, "Many are the plans in a man's heart, but it is the LORD's purposes that prevail." If you leave the planning to the Almighty God, then you are bound to succeed in His purposes, which is why you are here in the first place.

So how do we change our focus from being a puzzle

maker to that of a puzzle piece? A few steps in the right direction might look like this:

1) *Pray for God's purpose to be revealed*-If you don't know where you are supposed to fit as a piece of God's puzzle, pray earnestly for Him to show you. Even if you are certain that you are exactly where God wants you to be, still pray. He might want to change you and mold you in order to fit you someplace else. Either way, pray about it. Pray about your major, your internships and jobs during college, and your life direction after college.

2) *Take a look around you*-In your life, do all the pieces around you seem to fit? If not, it may be a good indication that change is on the horizon. Perhaps you will be moved (geographic location, your major, line of work), or perhaps pieces will move around you (friends, dating relationship, coworkers, or bosses). STOP and take a look at the pieces around you. Pray about them too!

3) *Move when you are called*-One of the worst things we can do is not move when God wants to move us. For the most part, we are afraid of change. When change comes from God, we need to be excited because it's a step toward His purposes. Listen to this promise in Jeremiah 29:11, "'For I know the plans I have for you,' declares the Lord, 'plans to prosper you and not to harm you, plans to give you hope and a future.'" The Creator of the universe has specific plans for you, and good ones at that. Let Him carry them out!

It's not easy being a puzzle piece, is it? While part of us would like to think that we can control life and call the shots, it's nice to know that our role has nothing to do with that very heavy burden. I encourage you to work with God instead of against Him. Be in prayer, look at the pieces around you, and be willing to be moved to where you belong.

A Few Words on Passion

What are your very favorite things to do? I love playing basketball, playing piano and guitar. I love being a waiter, speaking to audiences, and writing. These things are not my passions, they are just activities. A passion is the common thread that connects them. My passion is performing. Whether it's on the basketball court or in a restaurant where I can entertain people and laugh with them, I love performing. God wired me in a way that I receive incredible amounts of pleasure (and hopefully am a source of it for others) when I am performing.

You know what's funny? Many adults are struggling to pinpoint their passion. Perhaps part of the problem is how our culture interprets and answers questions. When we ask, "What do you do for a living?" we get the response of "I'm a nurse," or "an assembly line worker" or a "youth pastor". By the response we receive, one might think that we asked, "What is your job title?" This is not how it was when Jesus walked on earth. He didn't tell people that they would be evangelists, He said, "You will be fishers of men." That brings us to this point: The most important part of your life's work is not what your work is called, it's what your work does. If you are a nurse, you help sick people. If you are an assembly line worker, you put things together. If you are a youth pastor, you help connect the hearts of students with Christ. When you focus on what your work does instead of what it is called, the purpose and passion behind it are revealed.

What is your passion? Only you and God really know what it is. The way to find out is to search for the common thread in your favorite activities. The way to apply that to your life's work is to focus on what your work does, not on what it is called. Now, how does this fit in with choosing a major? The truth is that your major might or might not be connected to the things you truly enjoy. Now it's time to find out why.

A Major is Not a Career Path—It's a Skill Set

Many students do not understand the purpose of a major. Some college advisors are in the same boat. Most people believe that a major is a preview of a future career path. Therefore, those who major in accounting will be hired as accountants, biology students later become biologists, and English majors will seek a career in English. A major is not designed to limit your career opportunities. While some majors lead students toward specific roads of occupational opportunity (such as medicine, law, or education), most majors are not avenues to a direct career path.

A major is designed to sharpen a particular skill set. For example, one of my majors was finance. By studying stock valuation, corporate financial analysis, and derivative investments, I learned how to critically analyze situations, logically solve problems, and effectively measure results. These skills are applicable in many careers, not just occupations with a financial focus.

Consider King David, who was distinguished in the Old

Testament as being "a man after God's own heart (Acts 13:22)." David did not major in royalty. He majored in shepherding; with a minor in music (he played the harp). How did a young man with a very humble shepherd background emerge as king of Israel? While tending sheep, God gave him the experiences and training that sculpted David into a brave and God-fearing leader. God equipped him with the skill set of a king.

Question for you: How many people do you know that are currently working in the same field in which they received their degree? I challenge you to ask ten people about their occupation and their major. I would be surprised if 50 percent of the people you talk to are in a career directly related to their major in college.

From the first day of college, probably even before that, one of the most frequent questions you will be asked is, "What's your major?" While it is tempting to go and get a really sophisticated major just to have an impressive answer to that question, you are better suited by entrusting your area of study to the same God that had David study sheep before making him king. Take your time in picking your major because this decision will determine what skill set you sharpen in the classroom.

Navigating the road ahead, especially in regard to picking a major and a career, can be a challenging task. If you think about a major as being a sharpened skill set, you will put yourself in better position to find work that fits your passion. In the grand scheme of things, have faith in the fact that God is in control of your future, and what He has planned for you goes way beyond what major you choose.

Serve for a Summer

Now it's time to talk about the best summer(s) of college. As coveted as your summers will be (you only have three or four to use), you will want to give one away. The opportunity is so good that you'll jump at the chance. What is the opportunity? A summer spent serving God.

It seems like half of my friends from Campus Crusade for Christ at the University of Minnesota went on summer projects. They'd go to places like Ocean City, NJ, Orlando, FL, Lake Tahoe, CA, Indianapolis, IN, etc. At these summer projects, my friends would live with other students and staff directors from all over the country. They'd get a job, spend time in Bible studies, help in the community, and spend time sharing their faith.

Everyone that I know that has gone on a summer project has loved it. You meet great people (and have reunions frequently), learn a lot about yourself, and grow in your faith. It's like a Christian summer camp, but one thousand times better.

"Summer project is the best investment a Christian can make in themselves and in God. You grow and change, it's an absolute blast, and you meet friends for life," explained Nicole, a student at Penn State. "I went to two summer projects, and I wish I could've done three. Serving God is just contagious."

She's right. Serving God is contagious. A summer of service beats any internship, summer job, or vacation. I recommend it very highly, as do my friends.

How to Make the Most of your Work Experience During College

What would be your dream job in college? Thing big, now. Would you be a mascot for your college or university? Would you be an intern at a radio or television station? Perhaps you could work at the theatre, study abroad and work, or find a position in ministry in a different part of the world.

There is so much you can do to gain experience in different work areas while you are in college. The best part is that you have an opportunity to combine experience, fun, travel, class credit, and a payday with work.

One of my friends from Madison, WI had the coolest internship ever. Craig is a rock solid Christian who is getting his degree in civil engineering. In the summer of 2003, he worked in Athens, Greece with a construction firm that was building the Olympic Complex for the 2004 Games. He got to tour around different parts of Europe, learn about an entirely different culture, partake in an experience that would serve him greatly within his field of study, and grow his faith in the process. It was a blast for him!

"I remember going over there and thinking, 'Wow, this is a totally different culture.' They work a lot differently in Greece. It was a challenge to learn how to adapt your methods of doing things into their culture," Craig said. "In addition, I was able to see how vastly different their view God was in a foreign country. The Greeks are very passionate people in everything they do. If that whole country was turned on to Christ, they would be unstoppable."

What an invaluable experience that Craig was blessed

with. As you consider how you would like to use your time and work opportunities that await, it will be beneficial to pay attention to the following college work criteria.

Everything is ministry. There seems to be this idea somehow that if you aren't working in a church building, then you aren't doing ministry. Untrue. Jesus' disciples didn't spend much time hanging out in churches because that's not where the lost hung out. Every single work opportunity you will have during college will have a ministry opportunity tied in with it. Do you think God would send you into any situation without plans for you to have a role in growing His kingdom? Since God hasn't disowned this planet, everything on it is a ministry opportunity.

Think fun first. You have forty or so years after college to be plugged into serious sorts of labor. College is the last time when you can think fun first and practical second when it comes to jobs. Be a white water rafting instructor, work at Disneyworld. If you can train your eye to have fun and work during college, you are more likely to enjoy what you do after college.

Work on sharing your faith. This is a big one. When God uses you to bring someone to Christ it is incredibly exciting. But just like everything else, sharing your faith takes practice. There is a great book by Bill Hybels called *Being a Contagious Christian* that talks about sharing your faith. There is a great resource online at www.dare2share.org. In addition, the Campus Crusade for Christ website (See appendix) has tools about sharing your faith. If God is going to provide a job for you, I'm sure He'd like you to do some work for Him.

There are so many parts to getting the work you want during college. When you consider that everything is ministry, can think fun first, and work on sharing your faith, you'd be amazed at how many doors begin to open.

Your Future in a Nutshell

Time on this planet is short, and time spent in college is even shorter. How will you plan it out so that you maximize your experience? Most people stress out and get frustrated trying to plan out a life that isn't theirs to plan. Remember that you are a very prized piece in God's puzzle. He has a place for you. Additionally, take some time to figure out and apply your passion. Connect that passion, if you can, to that skill set called your major. And after you serve for a summer and grow closer to the Lord, invest the rest of your work time in college towards experiences that will provide the added richness during the college years that you were created to enjoy.

God has great plans for you. He's not going to call up your cell and clue you in. You have to get dialed into Him in order to learn of what He has in store. Let Him plan out your future, whether it is during college or beyond. He'll never lead you astray.

Things turn out best for people who make the best of the way things turn out.

John Wooden

There is surely a future hope for you, and your hope will not be cut off.

Proverbs 23:18

Chapter 11

The Final Piece of Wisdom: Cherish the Road Ahead

College has the potential to be one of the greatest times in your life. You will have an opportunity to experience your first steps of freedom and avenues to grow closer to God. You will be challenged in the classroom academically and spiritually. There may be an opportunity to experience the magic of a Godly dating relationship. In addition, you will learn how to grow closer to and increasingly appreciate family and friends. College will also provide a real life education about finances. You will also be introduced to once-in-a-lifetime opportunities, and those will help to prepare you for your future. From moment to moment, this can be one of the richest experiences life has to offer.

However, college is only what you make it. You can take this opportunity God has given you and minimize its positive impact. You can make decisions in a heartbeat that can significantly and negatively impact you for a lifetime. Just as much as college is full of opportunity, it is equally stocked with danger. Sadly, instead of walking with God diligently during college and experiencing His intended blessings, many walk away wounded.

Over 200 college students have shared with you the most important lessons they have learned. You have been armed with wisdom that will serve you greatly if you choose to apply it. Proverbs 4:11-13 says, "I guide you in the way of wisdom and lead you along straight paths. When you walk, your steps will not be hampered; when you run, you will not stumble. Hold on to instruction, do not let it go; guard it well, for it is your life." You have been given wisdom for the road ahead and I pray you will use it. I believe that your experiences will be greatly blessed. Cherish your steps down the road of college.

Appendix: Bits and Pieces to Make Your Life Easier

Laundry Instructions

Just to keep everyone from experiencing the same laundry disaster I went through, here's a quick scoop on laundry, compliments of my mom.

Whites—Wash them in warm water (not hot, hot might shrink them). The exception is socks; wash them in hot water with a detergent that has bleach so that your white socks can stay really white. Dry all whites on low heat because the dryers in residence halls are usually extra hot and may cook your shirts the way an oven cooks a cake.

Darks—Wash them in cold water, but be careful not to over measure on your suds because it's bad for your clothes. Then dry them on low heat to ensure that nothing shrinks.

Towels and sheets—Wash them weekly if you can, every other week at the least because of all the germs. Always wash them on cold; dry on low.

For good sweaters (and other fine clothes)—Read the instructions first! There may be special stuff to do like dry-cleaning or washing the item by itself. Typically, though, wash on delicate mode, and maybe tumble-dry if you feel lucky. If not, let them air-dry.

Don't forget to check your washers and dryers twice to make sure you didn't leave anything in them. Also, don't leave your clothes because people may like what you are wearing and take it for themselves. Finally…if you're going home, take a suitcase of clean clothes home whenever possible. It'll make your mom proud.

Useful Websites For Christian Living In College

www.campuscrusadeforchrist.com
Campus Crusade is a student ministry on many campuses

www.intervarsity.org
InterVarsity is a student ministry on many campuses

www.fca.org
Fellowship of Christian Athletes is a student ministry on many campuses

http://home.navigators.org/us/
Navigators is a student ministry on many campuses

www.insight.org
Pastor Charles Swindoll's site is full of tremendous sermons and FAQ's about Christianity

www.faithstart.com
Dynamic and broad resource for Christian living

www.heavensoft.com
Free Bible verse memory program

www.boundless.org
A Christian webzine for college students

www.discipleshipjournal.com
Bible in a year reading program

www.adamerwin.com
Resource for those transitioning from high school to college

About The Author

Adam Erwin was born in Bloomington, IN, raised in St. Louis, MO, and now resides in Minneapolis, MN. Though his choice to live in constant frostbite has confused his family greatly, Adam enjoys living in the same city where he earned his finance degree at the University of Minnesota.

When not working on writing projects, Adam enjoys speaking to youth, church, and parent audiences. He also enjoys playing many sports. His favorite sport is basketball, even though the skill of dribbling has a tendency to elude him. If not on the basketball court, baseball diamond, or golf course, Adam can be found in the weight room in an attempt to acquire a third-dimension.

Most importantly, in 1996 Adam responded to God's call that he accept Jesus Christ as his Lord and Savior. Since that time, Adam has not sinned. Just kidding! Rather, Adam's relationship with Jesus has dealt with forgiveness of sin. Jesus loved the people of this world so much that He died on the cross for the sins of mankind, Adam's included. (John 3:16) By praying to accept Jesus into his life as Lord and savior, Adam was able to receive the gift of salvation that comes only through faith in Jesus Christ (Romans 10: 9-13). Since 1996 when Adam made his decision to have a personal relationship with Jesus, life has been full of rich and meaningful experiences. As it turned out, God had a better plan for Adam's life than Adam did…and He still does.

If you would like to contact Adam for any reason whatsoever, please feel free to send email to adam@adamerwin.com. If, however, you fancy leaving voicemail messages, please call 612-379-8216. No matter what you do, please be on the look out for more of Adam's books from The Road Ahead Series. God bless!